THE AMERICAN STAKES

THE AMERICAN STAKES

John Chamberlain

CARRICK & EVANS, INC., NEW YORK

Designed by Robert Josephy

PRINTED IN THE UNITED STATES OF AMERICA
BY QUINN & BODEN COMPANY, INC., RAHWAY, N. J.

For my father

ACKNOWLEDGMENT

Thanks are due to the editors of *Common Sense*, *Fortune*, *Harper's Magazine*, *The New Republic*, *The Survey Graphic* and *The Yale Review* for permission to use material that first appeared in their pages

CONTENTS

THE AMERICAN STAKES

Whose State?

NO BOOK on politics can be worth its salt if the author lacks a clear notion of the origins and evolving nature of the State. For the State, like other human institutions, is conditioned, so to speak, by the centuries, and is capable of being used for human ends only within certain definite boundaries. Philosophical idealists such as Dorothy Thompson and Walter Lippmann frequently write brilliantly useless columns on politics because they either ignore or have forgotten the origin of State power in brutally unashamed force. And Marxists fail generally to understand the *democratic* State because they assume that the force of an owning class knows no limits and is always agreed on its aim. The philosophical idealist forgets that a human institution, having continuity, must preserve some of its original characteristics—which, in the case of the institution of the State, are wholly unlovely. The Marxist, looking at the naked power base of politics, forgets that original characteristics can be diluted and even transmuted by democratic custom and by the historical precedent of declared truces between classes that don't dare press the issue of power to its ultimate consequences. It is not always expedient for power blocs to

engage in totalitarian political warfare, but the Marxist
assumes that the class war must be increasingly totalitarian, with each side bent on the complete extinction
or captivity of the other. Assuming as it does that
wolves and deer can't live together in the same forest
because *some* wolves eat *some* deer, this view bears no
necessary one-to-one correspondence to the facts of
nature, or of human nature. At its best it describes what
can happen at intervals in the history of wolves and
deer, or in the history of human beings. But even at its
best it ignores the fact that a state of tension, even of
long-continuing tension, is just as "natural" as the
drive to make the earth safe for one species of animal
or one type of man. There need never be a victory.
Goethe said, "You must rise or you must fall. You
must rule and win, or serve and lose; you must suffer
or triumph; you must be anvil or hammer." But
Goethe was a romanticist, and Goethe lied.

It is the assumption of this book that no clear-cut
victory of any class over any other class is immediately
at hand so far as America is concerned. For in spite of
suffering and unemployment, and in spite of the failure
of dividends, all the classes in the United States have
either enough or the prospects of getting enough to
make totalitarian warfare on each other an inexpedient
thing. (Better to take a fall in the rate of profit than
make the hazardous attempt to enslave the working
class, and better to take a WPA job than raise the barri-
cades.) The democratic State, which is the result of

limited class, group and regional warfare, will continue to exist. But who will have the preponderance of control? What are the possible limits of regional, group and class action in our democracy? It is these questions which this book will try to answer.

But first of all, as a matter of establishing credentials, let us explore the origins and evolving nature of the State, particularly the democratic State. The philosophical idealist denies that the State originates in force; to him, as to his eighteenth century ancestors who knew little of anthropology, the State is the result of a social compact drawn up by free men in the dawn of time. By the terms of this compact the free man surrendered certain Rights in return for the guarantee of other Rights against the encroachments of his neighbors. Now, so far as the origin of the United States goes, there is a certain element of truth in the social compact theory. For the American union is actually the result of a social compact that was freely negotiated by the various states at Philadelphia in 1787. This social compact came into being through the instrumentality of men who were well versed in the theories of the French Enlightenment, which happened to be wrong historically but which were rationalizations of a valid human hunger. And once the historical "error" was acted upon at Philadelphia in 1787, it became true for our national government. The different governments of the contracting thirteen states were, of course, another story: they had originated in force—the force that had seized eminent domain from the Indian hunters and then defended it against late comers from Europe; and the subsequent force that cut us loose from Great Britain. Thus the United States government may be explained as the result of an amalgam of theories: it is a compound of force and of negotiated guarantees.

But the government of the United States was set up in the Age of Reason, and was something new under the sun. So far as early history goes, "the people" had nothing whatever to say in the making of the State. They were merely the dumb, uncomplaining hunters and diggers-in-the-ground who sat by and wondered when warlike nomads—herdsmen and sea rovers for the most part—created the State as a power-mechanism to insure tribute to themselves in the form of ground-rent. Before the creation of the State all people lived by the "economic means"—i.e., by the application of brains and brawn to the freely available raw materials of the earth's surface. But after the State had been set up, the insiders had one leg up on the rest of mankind, for their brand-new power-mechanism enabled them to live by the "political means"—i.e., by taking as tribute in the form of rent or taxes what other people had created by the economic means. We have come a long way since the formation of the first State, but the antique phraseology of our formal land deeds—which guarantee possession to those who are "well-seized" of their property—still testifies to the origin of land ownership in forceful pre-emption. The State was originally

14

the hand-maiden of this pre-emption: its arms of the law and the police and the military were dedicated to the defense of title to the choicest parcels of the earth's surface.

Franz Oppenheimer, who wrote in Germany at the beginning of this century, clinches the point with a great show of learning. Everyone is familiar with the organization of the Norman government in England: here the gangster origin of the State shows up in peculiarly crude outline. As Murray Godwin used to say, the gang of William the Conqueror muscled in on the Saxon earldom, took whatever sources of income they wanted for themselves, and prescribed the terms on which the older English population, the Celt-Roman-Teuton amalgam, might presume to exist. But the invasion of England in 1066 might be dismissed as merely *one* way of creating a new State. Alas for the philosophical idealist, however, the creation of the Norman State in England cannot be dismissed as either accident or exception: it followed a pattern which Oppenheimer has established as universal for all early history. In every case, whether among the aborigines of Dahomey or the Sudan, or in China of the Mongol and Manchu domination, or in the Japanese islands, or in Europe of the barbarian invasions, the State came into being when warlike nomads moved in on the unoffending ground-grubbers whose claim on the soil was a simple use-claim. The nomads had all the advantages of fiercer occupational characteristics: it took nerve and skill and extreme self-possession to ride herd on wandering flocks over the grasslands of the world. This nerve and skill easily enabled the nomad to set himself up as a feudal lord, the originator of "property" in the materials of production. Property forms have proliferated in many directions since the day of the Magyar invasion of Hungary or the Norman seizures of Sicily and England, but underneath the multiplicity are the outlines of the original simplicity: the State is set up to assure continuity and certainty to those who have forcibly established a prescriptive right of access to the earth's abundance.

To use Murray Godwin's phraseology, the State was created as a racket, with the major "take" from the land going to the warrior-gangster who could hang on to the political means of getting wealth away from those who used the economic means of bringing the wealth into existence. And in proving the case against the philosophical idealist who clings to the Social Compact theory of State origin, we have seemingly underwritten the Marxist axiom that the State is always at any given time the instrument—or the "executive committee"—of a ruling class. But the Marxist axiom is either a useless truism—the truism of "He who rules, rules"—or else it is false to the history that has been built on earlier history. The State, as Murray Godwin has said, is "a racket." But Oppenheimer has some interesting evidence to offer on permissible shadings of this conception: unlike Murray Godwin, unlike Marx, unlike the Lenin of "The State and Revolution," he recognizes that a racket can be a strict racket or a limited racket, and that continuity and certainty of possession may be made contingent upon other factors. In his reading of history Oppenheimer observed a countervailing tendency that makes strict rackets—or strict hogging of the materials of production—impossible to operate over long periods of time: human nature abhors the strict racket as much as inanimate nature abhors a vacuum. When the first wild herdsmen moved in upon peaceful ground-grubbers they killed them and rode away with the immediate spoils of the slaughter. These early nomads were the strictest racketeers of all, and Oppenheimer likens them to the bear who destroys the hive to get at the honey. But soon the first limitation on the racket appeared in the form of an exercise of common sense: wisdom dictated the cessation of totalitarian warfare against the grubber-in-the-ground. To some primordial thinker of genius it suddenly appeared a sounder tactic to imitate the bee-keeper and keep the hive intact for the future supply of honey. Hence the marauder became the guardian, levying whatever tribute the traffic would stand and "protecting" the hive against less considerate seekers-after-honey.

But even the feudal tactic was too strict a racket to work well. The serfs discovered they could make a better go of it by deserting the manor for the tradesman's town, and in some instances they were prone to bloody *Jacqueries* which made life a nightmare for the feudal lord who happened to be sitting on the discontented. When the "owning class" became sub-divided into a trading class and an agrarian aristocracy, there developed a natural rift in the techniques and the ends of ownership that makes the Marxist theory of two clearly opposed classes inadmissible: it is a theory that belongs in its essence to the feudal stage of history. The more intelligent feudal lords recognized the difficulty of continuing a strict racket once the property interests of commercialism and crude manufacture had grown to a point at which bidding for service set in. It was at this point in human history that the feudal baron discovered he could get better work out of his serfs if he fixed the tribute at a certain sum, letting the industrious underling keep the fruits of extra enterprise. In short, the racketeer discovered the law of diminishing returns as it applies to all forms of slavery or helotry; and the psychological groundwork for the doctrine of "natural rights" was laid in this simple exercise of reason.

When Rousseau and the other philosophers of the Enlightenment formulated the doctrine of the "social compact" and of "natural rights," they did so out of a complete misunderstanding of primitive history. It is true that among the Indian tribes of North America there were "confederations" based on the consent of the tribesmen, but the Indians had no State as we know the State, with a rigmarole of law, courts and police set up to maintain certainty and continuity of possession of the materials of production. However, it will not do to dismiss Rousseau as merely a dreamer, merely a wishful thinker. For Rousseau's *hunch* was sound: it was based on the historical truth that a strict racket always tends to break down. Possession may be nine points of the law; but when the helot loafs or grouses on the job the possessor's title can be made next to useless. The countervailing force of sheer human numbers will always tend to hobble the racketeer's power and put a boundary to his exactions. And at that boundary line will grow up a series of definitions of "rights." They are "natural rights" in the sense that they are grounded in an enduring, or at least a recurring, phase of human psychology. And, quite "naturally," they make the slave State an unstable equilibrium that cannot hope to endure forever as long as there is a "free" State—or a more limited racket—next door to set the helots an uneasy example. To the extent that he tried to invest his doctrine of "natural rights" with the authority of primitive antiquity, Rousseau was wrong. But Rousseau had a valid truth by the tail, even though he dressed it up in clothing that does not belong to it.

Karl Marx was deep in the study of the theory and practice of the strict racket when he evolved his philosophy of the State. He had read Hegel, who believed in the abstract "right" of the State to supreme power over the individual; he had observed the spectacle of feudal rule in Germany and Russia; and he had specialized in a study of the results of the French Revolution, which had swung away from its dynamic origins in the theory of "natural rights" to the strict racketeering of Thermidor and Napoleon. Living in an atmosphere of arbitrary definition and action, Marx is not to be blamed overmuch for a mistaken belief that the only counter-vailing tendency against oppression is the revolutionary tendency of the human race to replace one strict racket with another strict racket, if it gets the chance. In justice to Marx it must be said that he conceived the strict racket of the proletarian dictatorship as a humane thing, inasmuch as he proposed to let the entire work-ing class in on the "take." But in his definition of "class" Marx was indulging the vice of "least common denominator" thinking. This type of thinking assumes that A and B must act alike and possess the same philo-sophical values merely because they have *some* charac-teristics in common. Marx was all too prone to dismiss constitutional guarantees of "rights" as mere class maneuvers; he ignored the fact that such things as Magna Charta and the Petition of Right, once granted, become dynamic in themselves. For there are always people even among "owners" to whom freedom of thought, speech and experiment is at least as important as security, and these people will fight for "rights" regardless of class position or economic interest.

Because he assumed the proletarian class must con-tinue to act as a unit after the consummation of the Revolution, Marx never got around to the perplexing questions of vertical division within a class. He failed to see that freedom, to some proletarians as to some "owners," must seem a "good in itself," while to others freedom will be less important than security. Abstractly considered, the question of "freedom," or of "rights," should never arise in a one-class State: where there are no minorities there is no need of protection for minorities. But the theory of the "common will" of a class is a vicious theory that leads insensibly to strict racketeering on the part of whatever bureaucrats have the power to "interpret" their class mandate. This theory forgets that on the economic side of life there will always be problems involving the *sorting of the take*, which can be handed out immediately as consumer goods or reserved for use as capital goods. These problems must arise in any society, whether capitalist, communist or social democratic. The strict racket of the one-party proletarian dictatorship may prove oppressive simply by misusing the power to sort the take. Marxism failed utterly to guess that parties would inevitably tend to form (either legally or illegally) around conflicting ideas of industrial tempo, or the proper division of working class energy between city and country, or the virtues of ant psychology versus the lure of grasshopper psychology. In other words, the Marxian system makes no provision for the re-emergence of the limited racket notion on the far side of the proletarian revolution. Because Marx failed to see that groups and individuals will take sufficient courage from their numbers to struggle for variously conceived "rights" even within the orbit of a hypothetically one-party State, Stalin and his followers have had hastily to cook up the doctrine of the continuous purge to gloss the failure of Marxist theory and to make the "common will" remain ostensibly common. To such Procrustean lengths all strict racket theory eventually tends to lead. The Moscow trials, far from being an unfortunate aberration of Marxism, are exactly the sort of thing it *must* produce. They flow from the theory that the State is *always* the instrument of a ruling class, not a racket that has *always* tended historically to modification and limitation as "rights" are forced by the realization that strict rule is not only uncomfortable but incredibly difficult to maintain.

Now it may be argued, of course, that an instrument is an instrument even when its use is circumscribed by use and wont and the tacit threat of rebellion. But the point which Oppenheimer makes, almost in spite of his will, is that the countervailing tendency inherent in human numbers can make the State racket into something that even transcends the limited racket. For in a country of many regions and groups the State tends to lose its originally clear instrumental function and *mutates* into a fulcrum to be fought over by rival groups. The fulcrum may be used from time to time to support the crowbar of any one group or division of society that can bring sufficient pressure to bear: it can, so to speak, be leased. When the Republicans are doing the leasing the fulcrum will be used to support a pry by Big Ownership in the form of a Smoot-Hawley tariff or a lowering of taxes in the upper income brackets; when a Roosevelt is in power the fulcrum will be used to support a counter-pry by the common man. Harold Laski says that "in an unequal society, the power of the State has always been a means of oppressing those who are excluded from the privileges it protects." But if this were *always* true David Lasser would be unable to get anything for his Workers' Alliance, and Mr. Harry Hopkins would be an "instrument" or a "means" of Mr. Morgan. What Mr. Laski is obviously trying to say is that when a small, homogeneous group of people own most of the materials and means of production they are in a good position to refuse compliance when the fulcrum of the State is used against them. Their social power may be such that it overshadows State power in the hands of others. But if they refuse compliance they will have to "justify" the refusal by a *coup d'état* or by civil war, in which they *may* lose. The point is that the power of the State isn't theirs for the simple asking; they must first seize it and hold it against other groups and classes that have had a share in State protection under limited racket theory.

How much social evil has resulted in recent years from the Marxian strict racket theory of the State it is impossible to determine. But the damage has certainly been considerable. The Marxian may protest his belief in the temporary uses of parliamentarism, but he will inevitably be less interested in making the democratic forms work than he will be in proving that they can't work beyond a certain point. The Marxian is committed by his theory to a use of parliamentary institutions and free speech not as something good in themselves or because they are the needed instruments of people whose love of freedom transcends purely material interests, but merely as a sounding board or a theater for propaganda looking eventually to the strict racket of the proletarian dictatorship. In his fight to preserve and deepen democracy the Marxian is beaten before he starts. For by the very nature of his philosophical assumptions he is psychologically unprepared to fight for democracy beyond the point where his strict racket succeeds in capturing the State. He is by definition interested in class power, not in freedom or democracy.

Knowing this, the democratic liberal must come to distrust the United Front or Popular Front tactic at precisely the point where his Marxian ally begins to appear successful in capturing the leadership of the United Front movement. For at this point the question of the ends of the United Front comes to be more important than the means. The democratic liberal, who is committed by his nature to limited racket theory, will at once begin to ask uncomfortable questions. Is the United Front to be a mere prelude to the operation of the strict racket of the one-party dictatorship of the proletariat? Or is it truly a tactic designed to preserve democracy and the right to form parties around basic differentiating ideas no matter what the economic system? As soon as these questions insist upon an answer the United Front must split apart, as it did in Germany long before Hitler capitalized the philosophical rift between the limited racket liberals and the strict racket Marxists.

All of this may sound pretty theoretical. But it is fundamental to every single quarrel that is agitating liberal and radical groups at the present. Ramsay MacDonald may be said to have failed in England not because he was too much addicted to parliamentarism but because he distrusted the power of parliamentarism; without knowing it, he was a strict-racket philosopher. He really believed that the State was the instrument of the Tory Party, and that nothing could be done about it. The Communists and the Social Democratic bureaucrats (who were Marxists in their ultimate State theory, too) let Hitler slip into power in Germany precisely because they had long since refused to honor parliamentarism as necessary to liberty in *any* type of society: they assumed that parliamentarism was a mere face of capitalism and hence were beaten by their assumptions before they started to fight. In England, France and the United States Fascism is less likely to triumph not because the ownership of the means of production differs markedly from ownership in Germany, but simply because Locke, Rousseau and Jefferson have endowed the western peoples with a vision of the superiority of the limited racket over the strict racket. It was the observation of these philosophers that pressure always tends to tear the strict racket apart, while the limited racket, being flexible, can adapt itself to pressure.

The Rousseau-Jefferson theory of the State is, in essence, the broker theory of the State, and there can be no successful defense of what John Strachey calls the "bridgeheads" of peace, civil liberties and the standard of living except by a coalition of groups or parties firmly grounded in limited-racket, or State-as-broker, theory. To a not inconsiderable degree the future of democracy rests with our formal thinkers: if they can inculcate a belief that the State belongs to the people as much as to anyone else, then they will encourage the belief that the bridgeheads of peace, civil liberties and the standard of living can be held against the strict-racket aspirations of any special group. But if the theoreticians continue to popularize the belief that the State belongs solely to the capitalists, they will be encouraging, not revolt, but a dangerous passivity. The only sound slogan is, "It's *your* State!" Under that slogan you can raise a fighting army for the defense of "rights." Under any other slogan you merely encourage the growth of cynicism.

It may be too late to persuade the Marxians that their theory of the State is wrong insofar as it applies to the western democratic nations. But it should not be impossible to appeal to less dogmatic theorists of political power, both the ones who are committed to philosophical idealism and the ones who have been temporarily bemused by Marx. As a philosophical idealist, Dorothy Thompson, for example, laments the fact that the New

Deal has merely substituted one group of predatory interests for another. But since the State is the *result* of man's predatory proclivities, this is exactly what we must expect; the State must always be the reflex of an adjustment of power groups. The proper test of the State, from the liberal's limited-racket point of view, is not to be found in asking: "Does it favor someone?" It is bound to favor whichever group-coalition has won the election. The real test is: "Has the way been left open for *my* group to fight for what it conceives to be its rights?" If the way is still open, then we have democracy.

The mistake of the philosophical idealist is the common one of considering the whole as greater than the sum of the parts. To his way of thinking, the State is purely a Committee of the Whole, with a sole duty to something nebulously defined as the Common Good, or the Commonweal. The individual, under idealist theory, must bow when the Committee of the Whole speaks. But this conception of the State leads to a ridiculous perfectionism that denies the right of the representative to *represent*. When Senator X of Idaho, for example, fights for a law favoring the potato growers of his home state, the idealist is apt to betray impatience and ask: "Why can't Senator X be a *statesman;* why can't he subordinate his local interests to the good of the nation?" Superficially considered, the idealist demand makes sense. But the nation is not a mystical entity; it is the sum total of local interests. To Senator X, any in-

jury to his potato growers is incompatible with the good
of the whole. Senator X quite rightly considers that he
has been sent to Washington not to legislate in a vacuum
of universal "statesmanship," but to act as ambassador
for the home folks.

Again, the philosophical idealist frequently objects
that groups and classes as well as individual representatives fail to consult the Good of the Whole. It seems
monstrous to Dorothy Thompson that our labor leaders
should fight primarily for *labor:* she seems to think that
John L. Lewis should keep the demands of the *rentier*-
consumer in mind when presenting the demands of the
coal miners. But the rentier-consumers have their own
pressure groups, the leaders of which know quite well
that it is up to them to look out for themselves. Conces-
sions will follow in due course as the result of controversy, and do not need to come before.

Indeed, the pressure group, far from being the
loathsome thing that it is commonly accounted by the
philosophical idealist, is absolutely necessary to the
functioning of an industrial democracy. The pressure
group has long since become the new democratic unit,
the corporate age's analogue to the individual free-
holder of Jeffersonian times. No Good of the Whole
can be considered fairly representative unless it is the
result of compromising the demands of the various
pressure groups, which may be described as the watch-
dogs of democracy. It is perfectly true that a pressure
group, under democracy, must be prepared ultimately

to bow to a broker's conception of the Good of the Whole as a workable compromise among factions. But if labor, say, should interest itself first of all in the concept of the Nation, it would soon find itself taken into camp by more selfish forces. The good negotiator never shows his hand until the chips are down.

Integral to the continuation of democracy is the much maligned political "boss." Americans have been boss-haters throughout their history largely because they like to preserve that part of their folklore which tells them they are philosophical idealists about government. But the folklore is only a moral convenience; actually, when it comes to election day, Americans forget idealist jargon and vote along class, group and regional lines. Since our classes, groups and regions are multiplex, and our political parties necessarily few, the boss must be called in to do a brokerage job of compromise in order to bring party order out of chaos. Lincoln Steffens used to picture the political boss as the "representative of privilege," one whose job was to betray the common people into the hands of "the interests." But anyone who takes the trouble to dip into the welter of state or municipal politics will soon discover that Steffens is only partially right. In certain phases the boss may be Judas-betraying-the-common-people. But in other phases he may be Jesus-befriending-the-common-people. In any event he is not so much a force in himself as a focal point. He stands on the spot where the lines of force intersect. Whether one looks at Chicago or Podunk the result is the same: the boss is generally a specialist in estimating pressures and in "weighting" their importance by judging where money, propaganda and custom take precedence over simple votes. When the job of assessing the relative claims is done, the broker offers his compromise. If the offer is shrewd, the broker keeps his job: if not, he goes out in a landslide. If he charges too much in "honest graft" or plain theft for his services he will get a reputation for being corrupt. In good times people will put up with the expense of corruption; but when times are bad they will yell for "honest"—i.e., cheaper —government.

Lincoln Steffens, one gathers, was against the broker theory of the State; he wanted his bosses to be straight-out class representatives. The whole business becomes a little confusing at this point. How, one might reasonably ask, can you have political democracy if you or your group or your class lacks a mechanism through which to register your pressure? If you have demands to make that conflict with other people's demands there are only two courses open to you: either you go to open war against the opposing group or you call in a broker, a professional compromiser, a "boss," to fix things up on a bird-in-hand basis. Unlovely as the boss is in some of his tactics, you can't have a world of freedom without him: the right of a group to political broker-service is the only practicable alternative to the Gestapo and the concentration camp. For the boss permits political pressure to be absorbed; where he doesn't exist the pressure must either rip the social fabric apart (in revolution) or be contained (as in the concentration camp or political chain-gang).

In presuming to defend the boss one inevitably lays one's self open to the charge that one is putting a gloss on the status quo, or, more concretely, of defending Frank Hague. But a defense of the boss is no defense of Hague, or of Boston's Curley, or of New York's Tammany. Hague is a supreme example of the boss who has forgotten his function and become part of the pathology of democracy: he has ceased to register pressure (specifically, the pressure of a growing C.I.O.) and is attempting to be a dictator who presumes to prevent any new pressures from rising. When bosses arrive at such a point they are usually blown away in the next political overturn. The democratic process will not tolerate strict racketeering in bossism for long.

The implication of all this is that democracy is only possible in a society of various groups and classes, a society of many available alternatives. And it suggests this to me: that students of society should forget the political boss and concentrate on the pressure groups behind the boss. The labor union, the consumers' or producers' co-operative, the "institute," the syndicate—these are the important things in a democracy. If their power is evenly spread, if there are economic checks and balances to parallel the political checks and balances, then society will be democratic. For democracy is what results when you have a state of tension in society that permits no one group to dare bid for the total power.

Communists will call this a reactionary position. Fascists will call it democratic corruption and do-nothingism. Actually, in 1940 in the U. S., it is anything but reactionary or corrupt. For the labor union and the cooperative still lag far behind the business institute and syndicate in power; they must be built up. Limited racket theory leads, not to John Hamilton's or Glenn Frank's conception of Republicanism, but to a continuation of the sort of government we have had under the New Deal. For the New Deal has been built on a rejection of both the strict racket theory of the Marxians and the no-racket theory of the philosophical idealist. If Franklin D. Roosevelt had been a strict-racket theoretician out to serve his class and not a broker-politician interested in preserving democracy, he would never have felt the imperative to fight for a limitation on the pre-1932 political power of Big Ownership. Like Ramsay MacDonald he would have folded up at the first hint of adversity. Simply because he is a limited-racket theoretician, one who believes in the right of various groups to struggle for a shot at using the fulcrum of the State, Roosevelt has been of service to more people and more groups than any other president in recent history. The danger of Roosevelt comes not from his own philosophy of government but from theoreticians around him who sometimes use the vocabulary of strict-racket political philosophy. Thurman Arnold, for instance, is of two minds about the nature of the State. He believes in democratic procedure. But his metaphorical figure for good government is the board that controls an insane asylum. The figure is not reassuring. It is true that an insane asylum is devoted to the *comfort* of its inmates. But it is nonetheless a strict racket so far as the inmates are concerned; it does not believe in allowing them a voice in defining what comfort is. (There are no "natural rights" in Matteawan or Bloomingdale.) The insane asylum is not a democratic figure of speech, and politicians who use it as a touchstone can only help lead to the social disaster of the strict racket in government.

But when Thurman Arnold invokes the insane asylum he is probably kidding. The New Deal as a whole has shown a lively disposition to keep the State a "free" thing—free, that is, to the largest number of people. Like all States, the New Deal State is committed to a defense of property titles in both the materials and the means of production. But where the social power inherent in ownership is too highly concentrated, the New Deal has sought by legal means to redress the balance. It has been sensible of the fact that when access to the economic means of getting wealth is hogged by a small number of people, the only countering power which the dispossessed or the unlucky or the "unfit" may invoke is—State power. Philosophical anarchists such as Albert Jay Nock say that any increase in State power is anathema, that no good whatsoever can come of it. But this is not necessarily true. State power should be judged, not as something inherently evil, but evil only when it allows the political means of getting wealth to take on the trappings of vested right for the beneficiaries thereof. If State power is used to increase the average individual's social power—i.e., his power to create wealth for himself by exercise of the economic means of applying brain and brawn to raw materials—then it is justified. The New Deal has often slipped, but on balance I think it will be found that it has worked to spread the base of the social power of the many at the expense of the social power of the few. It has, however, reached the limits of its maneuverability; and there is a danger that its supposedly temporary invoking of the political means—in WPA, or in paying farmers out of other people's production to sabotage their own production—will soon take on the trappings of vested "right." The fight, in the future, will be over the question of increasing our total production instead of spreading what production we have. And the change in stress will inevitably bring new politicians on the scene. It may even cast the Democratic Party in a reactionary role.

Blocked Roads to Freedom

BACK in the days before Versailles, before the hopes of "good old 1913" (to use Elmer Davis's fond phrase) had gone glimmering with Woodrow Wilson's health, American liberals were far more conversant than they are at present with Grand Political Theory. On one level they read books like Herbert Croly's "The Promise of American Life," or Walter Weyl's "The New Democracy," or Walter Lippmann's "A Preface to Politics." And on another and more exciting level they listened while the anarcho-syndicalist philosophers who stood behind the I.W.W. movement quarreled amiably between trips to Paterson and Lawrence picket-lines with Debsian socialists about the uses and abuses of State power.

From a purely intellectual standpoint that was the golden age of the American radical movement, an age in which rifts between liberals, radicals, anarchists and socialists of various hues were hardly matters for blood-feuding and personal calumny. Socialists and anarchists naturally thought liberals were balmy, but it was taken for granted in that spacious period that one should use one's own mind; the "party line" had not yet been looped and knotted into a noose for the hanging and

35

strangulation of all who engage in heretical disputation.

With the entrance of the U. S. into the World War, the arguments either ceased or became rancorous mudslinging between patriots and Zimmerwaldists, Wilsonian Democrats and pacifist isolationists. The great days of the New Freedom and the New Nationalism, of Big Bill Haywood and Elizabeth Gurley Flynn and Carlo Tresca and Eugene Debs and Meyer London, were over and done. It is true that Randolph Bourne, the hunchback without illusions, carried on with High Theory even after George Creel's wartime propaganda bureau had tacitly signaled a halt to nasty cracks about war being the "health" of the State; but if we except Harold Laski, who quit this country for England after the suppression of the Boston Police strike, Bourne stands as the last figure on these shores to take the subject of Grand Political Theory with argumentative seriousness. There have been many books on aspects of politics since 1920; there have been translations of the systematic treatises of Pareto and Mosca and Karl Mannheim; there have been attempts to reduce politics to a behavioristic science (the work of Harold Lasswell and his followers); and there have been somewhat capricious personal essays on the order of Albert Jay Nock's "Our Enemy the State." But, in general, American liberals dropped Grand Political Theory for some twenty years. Few, indeed, are the intellectuals of the post-Versailles period who have shown the slightest interest in people like Henry George, Franz Oppenheimer or

Randolph Bourne, all of whom wished to isolate the factors which tend to make the State into an engine of suppression. And few indeed are the people now under forty who have ever opened the pre-war books of Croly, Weyl and Lippmann.

The reasons for the lapse of interest in Grand Theory are not far to seek. On the one hand, the Crolys, Weyls and Lippmanns had obviously overestimated the capacity of the free-wheeling liberal to harness the energies of various social power-groupings for the achievement of Utopia. And on the other hand, there seemed to be no use arguing about Marx, the Communist, or Bakunin, the Anarchist-Communist. The history of radical political theory seemed for the moment to be closed by the gigantic new Fact of the Bolshevik October Revolution. With one-sixth of the earth's surface under Soviet control, Lenin and Trotsky had seemingly proved the validity of their diagnosis, the realism of their particular Grand Theory. Anarchists such as Emma Goldman and Alexander Berkman might rage over the slaughter of the Kronstadt sailors, but anarchism had palpably missed the boat in Russia along with liberalism and the more genteel varieties of socialism. Outside of Russia the Social Democrats were proving powerless to push economic change to the point of socialist planning for all. Hence there seemed nothing for theory to do but to wait upon the outcome of what liberals were gingerly coming to term "the Russian experiment." Champions of anarchism, anarcho-syndicalism, Guild Socialism, Belloc-Chestertonian distributism, the co-operative movement, Fabian socialism and the old-fashioned social service State were all alike in being silenced by the pragmatic spectacle of Moscow and the first Five-year Plan.

The prestige of the Soviet Gosplan, or State Planning Commission, gained immeasurably in liberal circles from the obvious plight of western capitalism, which seemed unable to digest the aftermath of the World War. For, while Nazis fought pitched battles with Weimar republicans in German streets and England flounced off the gold standard and Mr. Hoover cracked down with an unimaginative fist on the bonus marchers and the breadlines lengthened in Detroit, Russian industry was compounding its growth at the unbelievable rate of twenty per cent a year. Electrification, which was in Lenin's mind the prerequisite for communism, had been pushed even before the period of the Five-year plans; by 1928 the capacity of Russia's central power stations had increased by fifty per cent. And from 1928 on to 1933, with the first Five-year Plan setting the objectives, geologists poked at the Siberian hills and factories went up in regions that had been wilderness. The Turk-Sib railway was finished, the Kuznetsk coal fields were opened, cotton was planted in Turkestan, wheat in Siberia. And American engineers, paid in newly-mined Soviet gold, took jobs in Russia for the sound capitalistic reason that they could earn more money there than at home.

Blocked Roads to Freedom

There was, of course, a lot of waste and confusion. The "paper-work" of planning for a sixth of the earth's surface and 160,000,000 people was endless; the "over-head"—or the "burden," as engineers like to say—was terrific. Russian peasants, only recently uprooted from a handicraft-vegetable economy, did not take easily to the manipulation of machines. The problem of making enough city goods to pass on to the peasantry in exchange for a continuous and broadening food supply had been skimped by the Bolshevik leaders, who were mostly of urban origin and sympathies. Monetary troubles came in the wake of negligent cost-accounting; Marx had written very little about money in a socialist society, and his Russian followers had not stopped to reckon with the fact that inflation could happen under communist circumstances. Moreover, the tempos in various sectors of the new Soviet industry tended to get out of alignment with each other, with the result that raw materials were not always ready for the factories, and vice versa. But up through 1932 the surface indications were all heartening to western liberals who were waiting on the outcome of the "experiment." Between the Russia of 1932 and the Russia that had been ravaged by civil war and fought over by White Guard adventurers and western interventionist powers before 1921 there seemed all the difference between Utopia and hell.

And then came the rude awakening, the first signs of really inefficient "back-tracking" in what was supposedly

the straight-line assembly flow of the great Soviet factory. Western liberals, who were expecting the moon on
a Soviet silver platter in 1932, had fantastically extrapo-
lated the curves of their hopes; and they were not psychologically braced to assimilate adverse news. Those
who had gotten a new, if secular, religion by looking at
Russia reacted to such things as the great 1932-33
famine, in which three or four million peasants died as
a result of inept handling of the drive for agrarian col-
lectivization, by a simple denial of statistics. The hard-
boiled liberal fringe murmured something about not being able to make an omelette without breaking eggs. And
still another group of liberals turned on the U.S.S.R.
completely. There could, so they said, be no hope in
central economic controls; and if Five-year-planning
needed a gay-pay-oo, then hurray for western confusion
and the old-fashioned trade cycle and Carl Snyder's
figures which "proved" that industry's natural rate of
growth was around three per cent per annum, not the
twenty per cent which was being rung out of the blood
and bones of Stakhanovite shock-workers in Mr. Stalin's
sweatshop.

Since they were born of a reaction to false hopes, all
the liberal attitudes of 1933-39 have been pretty silly.
As a matter of fact, Russia, which had to build from
the ground up in a razed, typhus-ridden land, has had
no validity as a laboratory of any sort so far as the west
is concerned. It had no validity even in the revolutionary period of 1918-21, when Lenin and Trotsky were

supposedly "proving" the case for revolution as against Fabian gradualism and reformism. In Germany and in other advanced industrial nations Communists have since discovered through successive defeats that Leninist revolutionary methods of "conquering" State power are archaic: one can't capture a vast congeries of public and private organizations situated in many populous cities by simple street fighting or by occupying the physical plant of a few factories. And as for the Russian economic planning, its problems are utterly different from those which face would-be planners in the west, where the primary task is to get full production and distribution out of a physical plant that already exists.

Recent Russian history has, of course, been prickly as a blackberry patch with barbarities. At least some of the bloodiness is due to Asiatic, or uniquely Russian, tradition. And some of it goes back to the fact that Russia has been a "ringed" State, fearful of attack from both east and west. In 1927, just before embarking on the first Five-year Plan, the Bolsheviks hoped to get capital from the western nations. But the capital was not forthcoming; Herbert Hoover summed up the attitude of the western financial community when he called Russia an "economic vacuum." Unable to borrow money for the purchase of capital goods, the Gosplanners were forced to divert most of the available Russian manpower from the production of consumer goods. And as a result of this, the Russian factory workers and city dwellers had nothing much to pass on to the farmer for his grain. When forced grain deliveries were resorted to by the Bolsheviks, the kulaks went in for passive resistance; they "forgot" to plant more than enough for themselves, or they killed and ate their cattle. The decision on the part of Stalin to collectivize the countryside naturally followed; and the famine followed later as the peasants stepped up their sabotage. In a western nation none of this might have happened; Gosplanning in the U. S., for example, would *begin* with the objective of flooding the countryside with city goods, and there would be no need of collectivizing the farmer, certainly not under forced draught.

Because Russia is *sui generis,* or just emerging from colonial status, it can be argued with a great deal of cogency that the experiences of the Bolsheviki are no test of socialism so far as Germany, France, Scandinavia, Britain and the U. S. are concerned. The "experiment" has been no experiment in the scientific sense that it can be repeated, for it was undertaken in circumstances that have no western parallel. Yet, in a larger sense, I think it is fortunate that liberals have been disillusioned with Russia. For, while the Soviets have proved nothing about the temper or the prospects for humanist advance that might be expected of a socialist experiment under western economic conditions, they have proved something about the workings of a one-party political system.

It is frequently said that human beings will only work at maximum efficiency for private gain. I cannot see that this is true: many people work out of motives of pride in the job, or of institutional loyalty, or of curiosity, or of simple habit. The enemy of socialism is not that all men have an ineradicable hidden yearning for profit; it is something more subtle than that.

A one-party political system can exist on the economic base of private ownership of the means and the materials of production: Germany, Italy and Chiang Kaishek's China, as well as our own Federalist Party period before 1800, have proved that. But there is no record that I know of in history of a two- or a multiple-party system existing in a State that owned all the land and productive equipment. The Incas tried communism; they also had theocratic rule. Democratic socialists will probably be quick to argue that State-ownership of all the means and materials of production need not prove oppressive provided the people are permitted to vote on their own planning program. But the State does not consist of a mass of atomistic, free-willed voters; it is a collection of institutions that tend to go their own gait, gathering power out of the sheer will to exist and to extend their fields of activity. An institution such as the Russian Politburo may "grant" a constitution, but as long as it has total disposal of the jobs needed to carry out the "democratically" agreed-on plan it certainly commands a patronage that is beyond the wildest dreams of democratic politicians. It may be granted that the "people" can set the goals for a Gosplan at the polls. But if the Politburo has the power of appointment and removal, managerial control is bound to express itself

43

from the top down. And such management can always coerce *future* voting by its command of present favors. *The "people," under such a system, must necessarily lack the free economic base for an opposition party.* Lacking this base, they must string along with the *de facto* bosses of the existing party. And they will, if they know what is good for them, vote for changes in the Gosplan which the bosses approve. If Stalin decides that Japan is menacing, labor-hours will be put into the manufacture of airplanes, not into the fabrication of badminton rackets or deck chairs. Stalin may be right about the Japanese, but the essence of democracy is that people shall have the right to go to hell in their own way if they want to.

Under western conditions of economic plenty, the will of the bosses might never prove oppressive: a samurai class, a materialist theocracy, of humane, disinterested civil servants might be developed. There would assuredly be no Moscow trials in countries whose legal traditions are founded on Anglo-Saxon respect for the individual. Yet freedom, as the west has known it, would be gone: the courtier virtues of deference and loyalty, and the courtier vices of fawning and intrigue, would replace the virtues and the vices of a capitalism that breeds both efficient production-minded industrialists and Wall Street buccaneers with impartiality. There may be no real choice between the virtues and vices of one system and the virtues and vices of the other. But if you don't like the courtier virtues and vices, you will

44

think twice about vesting *all* titles to ownership in the State. The right to oppose implies the right to make a living even in opposition; and if a dominant party controls all the means of production the right to make a living in opposition will be precarious, at best.

The Moscow trials clinched the case for me against complete State ownership of the means and materials of production. The squabbles underlying the trials have been dressed up as an Aaron Burr conspiracy for personal power, as a Japanese-Fascist plot, as a menacing intrigue to restore capitalism in the socialist fatherland. Yet, basically, all the quarrels proceeded from different conceptions of what should be the end and aim of the Gosplan. Trotsky wanted the peasants collectivized without any ado; therefore Trotsky went into banishment and exile. Bukharin, who had told the peasants to "enrich yourselves" in the NEP period, wanted Stalin to go slowly with the program for creating collective farms and artels; therefore Bukharin was bumped off. "Inner contradictions" had appeared in the U.S.S.R. for the simple reason—which should have been obvious all along—that members of the "classless" society were confronted with the same old savings-spendings dilemma that has always racked capitalist society. The State could hardly "wither away" as long as groups could argue about questions of industrial tempo, or of the uses of the available labor-hours. Even under conditions of complete socialist plenty Gosplanning must involve human choices; and the State apparatus has proved necessary to enforce whatever choice, whatever industrial frame of reference, the Politburo has seen fit to accept. So the problem of State power obviously remains under socialism; and the possibilities of oppression (of putting down those who, in the name of Trotskyism or Bukharinism or what-not, want different Gosplanning for different aims) remain, too.

The Moscow trials were dramatic evidence of a socialist horn to the age-old dilemma of blending freedom and economic security. The capitalist horn exists for the well-known reason that competition, at least in fields that require large blocks of capital, proceeds toward monopoly as depression shakes out those enterprisers who are not well-heeled. The socialist horn exists for the more obscure reason that complete State-ownership of the means of production makes it impossible for the Bukharins and the Trotskys to discover an independent economic base for an opposition organization. So there you have it: capitalist-Scylla and communist-Charybdis if you want both freedom to shoot off your mouth and freedom to make a living. The Populists, the pre-war Progressives of 1912, the Single-taxers and the Wilsonian Democrats always knew that; but they have been in the intellectual doghouse since the war.

In recent months, however, American liberals have been groping toward the realization that Marxism is not a complete lexicon of progress. Western planners— see the files of *Plan Age*—have developed a technique which can, I think, best be described as the technique of limited, or partial, planning. This technique does not require dictatorial control of the means and materials of production, for it begins by research and ends in the consulting chamber, with all claims—the claims of management, the claims of labor, the claims of ownership—represented in a final compromise. The planners are not the bosses nor are they rubber-stamps for the bosses; they merely act as advisers. And the various power-groups under democracy are permitted both to propose objectives—and to veto them if the road to attainment promises to prove costly.

The realization that Marxism· is not enough has caused many western liberals to check their sights in the past year or so: witness the recent spate of "democracy" books by Herbert Agar, Arthur Garfield Hays, George Counts, Mordecai Ezekiel, Max Lerner, Alfred Bingham and Maury Maverick. Later on I shall return to this portent, which has gone almost unnoticed. And I shall also return to a phase of the Russian "experiment" that has been overlooked by those liberals who took Lenin's word for it that the NEP period—or the period of the New Economic Policy that lasted from 1921 to 1928—was a "strategic retreat." But before grappling with NEP and the latest efforts of liberals to drive a course between a capitalism that makes for monopoly and a socialism that makes for monolithic party government, there are all the nineteenth century compromises to deal with. Anarchism, anarcho-syndicalism, Guild

Socialism, distributism and the co-operative movement have all seemed to promise, at times, a form of society in which neither economic nor political monopoly would be possible of achievement. Some of these compromises build on a communal ownership in which title to productive equipment and land rests with the group—say, with the labor union, or with the farmers' producer-co-operative. Some frankly build on a more traditional private property base, although all of them reject the property rights of that fictitious legal entity, the great corporation. What have these philosophies to tell us? Are any of them valid today? Let us see.

Bertrand Russell, in his "Proposed Roads to Freedom," finds good anarchist doctrine in the works of Chuang Tzu, a Chinese mystic philosopher of 300 B.C. who believed in abolishing all forcible constraint of the individual by the community. Probably Chuang Tzu's anti-Statism was old even in its time; indeed, anthropologist J. Leslie Mitchell would have us think that anarchism dates back to Old Stone Age times—to that "long Spring of the human race" when man recognized "no rule, no authority, no chief, no council of elders, no law, no sexual problems, no wives, no husbands, no gods, no devils, no science, no war, few irrational hopes and possibly fewer irrational fears." Modern anarchism, however, has a less happy genealogy. It is true that it looks back for its psychological warrant beyond the "struggle for existence" to a pre-historical period in which mankind was less a creature of tooth and claw than he was a devotee of mutual aid. But modern anarchism, which combines its fear of the State with a somewhat incongruous belief in community ownership of land and productive equipment, is, like modern socialism, an offspring of the industrial revolution. As such, it can only be understood by setting it against the background of European history of the nineteenth century.

Specifically, one must go to French nineteenth century history if one is to appreciate the forces which generated and amplified modern anarchist doctrine. In contrast with British nineteenth century history, with its long upward glide from Chartist hunger to Victorian richness and complacency, French nineteenth century history prior to 1871 consisted of spasmodic alternations of semi-dictatorial regimes and sudden, fierce popular uprisings that seemed to lead nowhere in particular. The intellectual reflex of such a state of affairs prolonged through three agonized generations was a straw-grasping Utopianism as to political ends, and a belief in violence as the only valid political means. French literature of Orleanist times—1830-48— abounded in the sort of thing which Edward Bellamy has made familiar to Americans in his "Looking Backward," a romance of the almost-perfect State. This, in itself, was harmless enough; but with such tantalizing dreams held before their eyes other Frenchmen— Auguste Blanqui, the Babouvists—were in a perpetual insurrectionary hurry to topple the government and bring about the Great Day at once.

Neither the Utopians nor the Blanquists were anarchists. Yet the society that spawned them was spiritually hungry for a freedom that is commonly denied by most governments, even including the democratic. Somewhat apart from the Utopian readers of Etienne Cabet's *"Voyage en Icarie,"* and quite, quite far distant from the insurrectionists, there stood the followers of Pierre Joseph Proudhon, the theorist of "mutualism." Proudhon has been called the "father of anarchism." He believed in the free association of individuals in economic communes; and he spent a decade of exile protesting against the dictatorship of the upstart Louis Napoleon. Yet, as Max Nomad has pointed out, he was a peculiar anarchist in that he believed in abiding by the law. The Proudhonian mutualists considered man a moral, rather than an economic, creature; and Proudhon himself set pure anarchism down as a distant goal to be achieved when mankind was morally ready for it. Meanwhile, what he hoped for in the present was a growth of mutual credit societies and co-operative industries, all federated in a loose check-and-balance State that would permit more freedom than France had known since the collapse of the hopes of the Great Revolution of *"liberté, égalité, fraternité."*

Into Orleanist France there strayed the real father of modern anarchism, the Russian Michael Bakunin. Bakunin came from an old aristocratic family: his father "owned" 3,000 serfs; his great-uncle on his mother's side was General Muraviev, the notorious "hangman of Warsaw" who had broken the Polish revolution. At the age of fourteen Bakunin was sent to the Artillery School in St. Petersburg; his father, who had changed his mind about liberalism after the failure of the Dekabrist conspiracy of 1825, was bent on rearing his children as loyal subjects of the Czar. After his graduation into the Czar's officer corps, the young Michael spent two years with his regiment in Minsk province, where he witnessed the suppression of the Polish uprising of 1830. That spectacle gave him his bellyful of authority; accordingly, he quit the army to study philosophy in Moscow, in St. Petersburg and on his father's estate in Tver.

It was a moral objection to coercion, not any theory of economic development or historical change, that brought Bakunin through his stage of "Hegelian fever" to anarchism. He was, however, a long time on the way to mature formulation of his beliefs. After leaving Russia he spent some time in Germany, which was then seething with the rebellion that led to 1848. Contact with the Forty-eight spirit made him into a revolutionist in a vague sort of way. When the Saxon police became interested in his first famous revolutionary apothegm, "The zeal for destruction is at the same time a producing zeal," he moved on to Switzerland, and then to Paris. It was here, on the eve of the *coup d'état* that was to unseat Louis Philippe, that Bakunin met Marx and Proudhon, whose respective philosophies he used as quarrying grounds for the doctrine that came to be known as anarchist communism. Indeed, modern anarchism might be expressed in a formula coming straight from the Paris of 1848: Marxian class struggle, plus Proudhonian mutualism and anti-Statism, plus a trust in the Blanquist insurrectionary deed, equals the anarchism of Bakunin.

In later years, after the suppression of the hopes of 1848 all over Europe, Bakunin quarreled bitterly with Marx. The quarrel was partly temperamental; but it was also (though disciples of both men will deny it) a question of patriotism. Bakunin hated German rigidity and order; he therefore distrusted Marxian socialism, which put its emphasis on the conquest of State power. Marx disliked Slavic dreaminess; he therefore read nonsense into Bakunin's theories. As early as 1848 Marx's paper, the *New Rhinish Gazette*, spread the libel that Bakunin was a Russian secret agent. The libel was later retracted; in any event it would have seemed silly in the light of Bakunin's subsequent prison sentence and exile at the hands of the Czar. But the enmity between Marx and Bakunin persisted through a lifetime of jockeying for the control of the revolutionary labor movement and the first two workingmen's internationales.

Never a precise doctrine, anarchism evolved in several directions after Bakunin's death in 1876. At one extreme were the anarchists who believed in the *attentat*, the propaganda of the deed: these included Johann Most, who put his trust in a slug of dynamite in a piece of lead pipe; Alexander Berkman, who tried to kill Henry Clay Frick; and possibly Leon Czolgosz, the assassin of President McKinley. These were sincere, if deluded, men, as the autobiography of Emma Goldman offers abundant testimony. Their terroristic doctrines shaded into the individualist anarchism of the people whom Max Nomad has called "crooks with a philosophy"—criminals who used anarchism as an ideological cloak for thievish and murderous desires. At the other extreme there was the gentle philosophical anarchism of Benjamin Tucker, who died just the other day in Monaco. Neither the anarchists of the deed nor the anarchists of the philosophical ivory tower, however, constituted the real strength of the movement after Bakunin's death. That real strength was to be found in the Italy of Errico Malatesta and the Spain of the martyred Ferrer, where the doctrine called anarcho-syndicalism made great headway in the trade union movement. It was to be found in the United States of the I.W.W. upsurge. And, above all, it was to be found in the ranks of the advanced trade unionists of France, whose doctrines of revolutionary syndicalism made all good people tremble in the days before the World War.

Syndicalism has been called the "anarchism of the market place." Like anarchist communism, it was a response to specifically French conditions; indeed, its name derives from the French word for trade union, which is *syndicat*. In England and Germany, the growth of the trade union movement coincided with the growth of social democratic and laborist politics. In France, however, the labor movement could make no use of political action; it found itself crushed to earth with every political upheaval from 1791, when it was actually suppressed in the name of the great French Revolution, to 1871, when the bloody defeat of the Paris Commune was synonymous with the defeat of all labor. Even after the birth of the Third Republic French trade unionism had to wait some thirteen years before the liberal ministry of Waldeck-Rousseau got around to legalizing it in 1884. With a century of defeat behind it, French labor regarded parliamentary action with an unmitigated cynicism that was pardonable in the circumstances.

If socialism had been able to get a strong foothold in late nineteenth century France, it might have pulled the trade union movement along with it into politics. But French workers outside of the industrial and mining districts of the north and northwest distrusted the socialists as much as they distrusted the possibilities of democratic political action. The reason for this distrust derived from the sectarian nature of French socialism, which revived under the Third Republic only to split itself four ways among the Marxian followers of Jules Guesde, the "possibilists" of Paul Brousse, the Allemanists, and the independent socialists led by Jean

Jaurès, Millerand, Viviani and Briand. And when Millerand, Viviani and Briand all deserted socialism for political careerism in the Center and on the Right, the distrust of the French trade unionists was compounded. . . .

Whether the slogan "no politics" amounts to anarchist politics is a question one might well refer to the Sphinx, or to the oracle at Delphi. Certain it is that Fernand Pelloutier, an anarchist communist, was the father of revolutionary syndicalism and the creator of the Fédération des Bourses du Travail, which coalesced with the Confédération Générale du Travail in 1902. Dominant in Pelloutier's "anarchist politics" was the idea of the general strike, the "strike with folded arms," which, in Sorelian terms, was the great energizing "myth" in pre-war labor in France. Local strikes, in the anarchist politics of the syndicalist movement, were the market place substitute for the old-time anarchist propaganda of the deed; the general strike was the equivalent of the Marxian revolution and was to result in the autonomy of the trade unions in free association with each other.

Inasmuch as pre-war France was still a country of small industry, syndicalist organization developed as a curious mixture of regionalism and national industrial unionism. Regionally, each single, separate *syndicat* was identified with a *bourse du travail*—a local chamber of labor that functioned for job-seekers and job-holders very much as the chamber of commerce does for business men. But each single, separate *syndicat* was also identified with national labor in its particular field through representation in the Confédération Générale du Travail. The C.G.T., after its merger with the stronger Fédération des Bourses, became a sort of parliament of labor, with representatives from the local bourses sitting on one side of the House, and representatives of national unions, both craft and industrial, sitting on the other. An Executive Committee of the Whole was formed by joint session of the two branches. The theory behind the two groupings was that each would tend to correct the other's point of view. As a matter of history, French labor localism was doomed to lose out in the post-war years; the idea of regional autonomy for labor was compelled to make its last stand in Spain, an industrially laggard country inhabited by the fiercest individualists in the modern world. . . .

Since it is a negation of organization, anarchism has never produced a body of theory comparable to that of Marxism: one can't write formal tomes about nebulous feelings. Bakunin's ideas are vague on the positive side; and Georges Sorel's are hardly constructive. The nearest thing to an anarchist theoretician is Peter Kropotkin, the Russian prince who dreamed a noble dream of factory work carried on in pleasant conjunction with mental labor and labor in the fields. An enemy of the international capitalism of Richard Cobden and John Bright, Kropotkin correctly foresaw that the "perfect" world division of labor would not survive the extensive export of capital goods and the costs of ocean-borne cross-hauling of products that might just as well be produced at home. But Kropotkin carried his animus against a division of labor to fantastic extremes: he wanted every intellectual and professional to do some farming or factory work (a good thing for writers, but a waste of a good surgeon's time), and he wished peasants to spend at least a few hours daily at the lathe or the work-bench.

Reading Kropotkin's "Fields, Factories and Workshops," one gets a sense of a curious mixture of medieval reversionism, William Morris estheticism, and high common sense. Long before the formal invention of "agro-biology," long before Stuart Chase started writing about "tray agriculture," Kropotkin found practicing agro-biologists in the market gardeners of the Paris suburbs. These gardeners, he noted, practically created their own soil; indeed, they fertilized to such an extent that they could afford to sell an inch or so of topsoil every year. From this observation it was just a step to the conclusion that "nations can live at home"— or that individuals, given a plot of earth, can live anarchistically provided the tax collector is lenient.

Most of Kropotkin's examples of happy peasants who combined farming with shop work, however, were drawn from backward regions of France, Germany, Switzerland and Russia: Kropotkin's view did not comprehend the world of stream-lined trains, continuous

57

strip-mills, four-lane highways and mass-production assembly lines. Not that a union of agriculture and assembly belt work is fantastic; Henry Ford, in his own paternalistic and most un-Kropotkinian way, has demonstrated that. But industrial development in a world of nationalist States, which creates great *de facto* power-units, renders the anarcho-syndicalism of one country the natural prey of the State capitalism of other countries. Anarchists bemoan this as a fact; but few of them are clear-sighted enough to admit that the anarchist creed has no chance on a continent or in a world that is cut up into squabbling nationalist strips.

Bakunin correctly foresaw the future when he labeled Bismarckian Germany the prime enemy of the anarchist movement. For when Bismarck took the petty German principalities and fused them into a powerful nation under the leadership of Prussia, he put the centralized State squarely at the service of the industrial revolution on the whole European continent. Thus, by one of those syncopated historical movements that make the neo-Marxian "law of uneven and combined development" a very real thing, anarchism and syndicalism were put on the defensive from a *national* as well as a class standpoint—a nasty paradox which no good anarchist has ever been able to surmount.

The hopelessness of the anarcho-syndicalist cause in a nationalist world was finally demonstrated by Spain. Had the Germans and the Italians kept their murderous paws off the Spanish peninsula, the anarcho-syndicalists, who were more numerous and certainly more indigenous than the Spanish communists, might conceivably have turned the Spanish Civil War into a victory for the libertarian philosophy; at the very least they might have been able to go on living as part of the trade union movement of a republican Spain. But, with Italian troops and German matériel against them, the soldiers of the Spanish Republic were compelled to accept a discipline that is incompatible with anarchism. Had the Republic won the war, anarchist ideas would have been partially discredited, though individual anarchists would have been honored for a courage that impelled some of them to fight against the Fascists with quite literal bare hands. But, the war being lost, it will be a long time before anarchism in Spain lifts its head to receive a tribute to either courage or ideology.

Spanish anarchists did, indeed, succeed in running factories and farms as "free communes" in the midst of war. But if they proved their point that group "ownership" of the means of production is possible, they also proved by their inability to key their productive efforts up to war-time pitch that Proudhonian mutualism is not for a war-torn world.

Even from the purely internal standpoint, anarchism and anarcho-syndicalism present a half-finished picture. Fearing power, anarchists think of the "revolution" as the day on which economic "rights" will be calmly assumed by the trade unions; they believe in the control of the economic processes by the producers. But

59

anarchist economics is a defective science, for it ignores the plain fact that many economic activities are interstitial, a matter of relations between primary and secondary producers, or between producers and consumers. When syndicates seized factories in Italy in 1920, they kept them going until they suddenly discovered that raw materials were necessary at one end of a process, and salesmen at the other. The organization of production does not necessarily require a government, as the Swiss Family Robinson discovered. But the organization of exchange demands some parametric device—say, a money system or a national accounting system—and this presupposes a State to create and enforce the common acceptance of the money or accounting medium. Anarchists and anarcho-syndicalists have never come to grips with the interstitial requirements of round-about production; and one book, Veblen's "Theory of Business Enterprise," is sufficient to blow a hundred years of anarchist thinking sky-high. Moreover, even if interstitial economics were not important, anarchism and anarcho-syndicalism propose to leave power kicking about in the streets, a huge, wildly threshing live wire. The power is there for any courageous—or even yellow-bellied—condottiere with a pair of rubber gloves to seize, as Mussolini proved in post-war Italy.

It will not do, however, to close a discussion of anarchism on a note of belittlement. For what is valid in anarchism and anarcho-syndicalism has been taken over or discovered independently by other movements

—by the C.I.O., for instance, or the co-operative movement. The industrial unionism preached by John L. Lewis is a syndicalist idea; and when the Swedish consumer co-operatives, for example, went in for manufacturing their own electric light bulbs they were taking a leaf out of Proudhon and practicing "mutualism." Again, the "vagabond wage" which some anarchists have proposed is gaining the status of a "right" even under capitalism: few governments permit the unemployed to starve outright, and just the other day it was seriously proposed that bread be made a public commodity, like water. Finally, the curious mixed regional-industrial organization of French syndicalism contained the germ of the British Guild Socialist movement, most promising of the pre-war roads to freedom.

One hears little of Guild Socialism these days: like Rupert Brooke and T. E. Hulme and Tony Wilding, the great Australian tennis player, it was a casualty of the World War. Yet, like other good things the war killed, it is deserving of its occasional hour of tribute; maybe, even, of resurrection. A social doctrine which once enlisted the crusading zeal of Bertrand Russell and G. D. H. Cole, humane men with uncommonly clear minds, cannot be wholly negligible even in radically new circumstances. When American newspapermen created the organization which they called the American Newspaper *Guild* they paid an unconscious compliment to the British movement which was then all but forgotten. I have heard the word "guild" criticized as being too fancy; "union," so the argument runs, ought to be good enough for reporters if it is good enough for steam-fitters. Yet such an argument is evidence of an inverted proletarian snobbery; and newspapermen don't need to apologize. Not only does "guild" connote a respect for craftsmanship, it also connotes a desire to control the methods and issue of one's work against the claims of private employer and State employer alike. As a word, it is stand-up, unservile.

Britons, so the old saw has it, never, never will be slaves. One sometimes wonders, these days. Yet Guild Socialism, with its insistence that security without freedom is a six-foot cell, arose as a typically British compromise between the claims of the pre-war socialists, who wanted to rest their heads forever in the lap of Mother-State, and the 1910 syndicalists, who had the quaint idea they could snub the State out of existence. As Cole has said, both socialism and syndicalism are right in what they emphasize and wrong in what they exclude. State socialism (and do we know any other?) may get its initial impetus from the trade unions, but it winds up, as in Soviet Russia, with the claims of the community—i.e., the consumers—taking precedence over the claims of individual trade unions, which are forbidden to strike against the terms of the Gosplan. Syndicalism results in the opposite social fallacy: it gives all to the producer (as in the anarcho-syndicalist communal undertakings in Spain), who is thus at liberty to hold up the community as a whole. To a logical people such as the French, the issue might appear insoluble; it is certainly not solved by Georges Sorel and the Revolutionary Syndicalists, who in point of fact were content to rest on a theory of Permanent Class War that is very much like Trotsky's theory of Permanent Revolution. To a logical mind it must seem that man, as both consumer and producer, must be eternally at war with himself, wanting to get more goods for less effort at the same time that other people, organized as the community, want him to get less for more. But the British have never been impressed by logic; they are used to bridging the unbridgeable, as the Statute of Westminster (does it free the dominions?) and the British Crown (is the King a cipher?) both go to prove. And, as we shall see, Guild Socialism arose as the natural British bridge between the unbridgeable claims of both State socialism and syndicalism. In Guild Socialism, Marx and Bakunin came to inhabit the same body —a miracle which, but for the World War, might have had a long shot chance of becoming for radicals what the miracle of Holy Communion is for practicing Christians.

To understand the genesis of Guild Socialism we must go back to England of the very earliest years of this century. The period of revolutionary Chartism and Owenite aspirations toward a millennial socialism had long since been forgotten; the trade unions, organized nationally, had shaken down into "pure and simple" mechanisms for wage-and-hour bargaining; socialist politics had become simple labor politics, an adjunct of British liberalism called lib-labism; and with the passage of welfare legislation of one sort or another political action seemed to promise enough to keep everyone relatively happy. The Fabian Society—organized Sidneywebbicalism, as Mr. Punch called it when contrasting the Webb doctrines of socialist "permeation" with the doctrines of French syndicalism—had long since enlisted the intellectual allegiance of most British radicals, including George Bernard Shaw. "The inevitability of gradualism"—how pat the phrase came! Yet, around 1910, something called the Labor Unrest made itself felt, and shortly this Unrest had attained to the dignity of a national bogy. Gold floating up to England from the Rand in South Africa had steadily expanded the British currency; prices had risen; production had increased; but wages lagged steadily behind. Gradualism or no gradualism, British labor stirred; its rank and file listened confusedly to echoes floating across the Channel, echoes of syndicalist Direct Action; Mr. Tom Mann, who had really read Sorel's "Reflections on Violence," was putting the direct action gospel to the test in the Scottish and Lancastrian north; and as strike followed strike in the years after 1910 the British middle classes—including the despised "salariat" which refused to take its place beside the proletariat—trembled at the vague possibility of a great General Strike. According to George Dangerfield, who has written eloquently of the period, that general strike, Sorel's "vital lie," was actually scheduled for September, 1914, when suddenly the World War intervened. . . .

Meanwhile, some Britishers had been doing a bit of thinking. Not the Sidneywebbicalists, who had done their intellectual pioneering back in the Eighties; not the Ramsay MacDonalds and the Philip Snowdens, socialists who tended secretly to deplore the Unrest; not even the Tom Manns, who were so immersed in the class war that they had no time for the peace conference that must follow all wars. Thought stirred in the mind of Hilaire Belloc, who feared the Servile State notions of both the Sidneywebbicalists and the capitalists who were more and more shuffling in the direction of a State Capitalism that could not have been vastly different from Mr. Webb's desired government by a Bureaucracy of Permanent Socialist Undersecretaries. But Mr. Belloc, who wanted to hand ownership of the means of production back to a wide variety of individuals, could not quite tell Englishmen how they were to slice a corporation like a cake; and his preachments were generally discounted as a Catholic reversionist's nostalgia for an England that had once dressed in Lincoln green. Mr. Belloc's fear of the Servile State, however, found itself echoed in quarters that had no fear of the corporate form of activity known as the trade union; for in the Middle Ages there had been workers' organizations known as guilds which had had full control over their own fate. . . . Why not, so certain Englishmen started to ask themselves, why not let modern industry be controlled by the trade unions reorganized as national guilds? This form of Group Capitalism (it was not called that at the time) would avoid both the uncertainties of private capitalism and the slavery involved in having only one employer, the Master State.

Guild Socialist doctrine was pieced together from many seemingly antagonistic sources, from Belloc to Marx, and from William Morris to America's Big Bill Haywood, who believed in industrial unionism. To Mr. A. J. Penty goes the credit for recovering the word "guild," although Mr. Penty, a medievalist, held out for a long time against modern industrialism, which was the thing all the other guildsmen were trying to save by giving it a new direction and a new control. The main driving force behind the idea, however, was French syndicalism as it was filtered through British understanding—specifically, the British understanding of A. R. Orage and his associates on the *New Age* and G. D. H. Cole and the members of the National Guilds League. Bliss was it in that dawn for Mr. Orage and Mr. Cole to be alive; they had not yet succumbed to the acids of age, the one to fall heavily for the Social Credit panacea of Major C. H. Douglas, the other to become (with his wife) a writer of detective stories.

To both Cole and Orage, syndicalist emphasis on the producing interest was a breath of cool air after three

decades of Fabian propaganda about the State being a
vast association of consumers. Fabian collectivism
seemed to exalt man in his *average* capacity as an eater
of food, a wearer of clothes, a taker of baths. Syndicalism, on the other hand, exalted man in his unique occupational characteristics. Pride was all on the side of the
syndicalist; after all, a man is far more apt to glory in
his ability, say, to hit sixty home runs a year or to do a
good job of design than he is to boast of his capacity to
eat steak. But pride (which was one of the seven deadly
sins in medieval times) can easily become anti-social;
and Mr. Cole and Mr. Orage set themselves to com-
puting the exact point at which the producer interest
must conform to the demands of sociality, or the
consumer-community.

The question of ownership was the biggest nut to
crack. If the union, or the national guild, was to own
land and capital goods outright, there would be nothing
to prevent a scramble on the part of each separate group
to get more of the means of production for itself. On
the other hand, nationalization of property in the means
of production might result in exploitation of the guilds
by the State: a governing bureaucracy might decide to
set inhuman or at least distasteful work tempos, or to
build up an unwanted new investment in plant at the
expense of the people's leisure. The guildsmen solved
the problem (on paper, at least) by agreeing to vest
title to land and capital with the State, but the guilds
were to lease this land and capital back for a rent just

large enough to cover government expenses. From his niche in Valhalla, Henry George, the Single Taxer, must have applauded this particular dodge that abolished both the unearned increment of private renting and the inequities of a variegated tax system in one clever swoop.

Politically, guild society structure was to be a combination of vocational, or functional, representation and an old-fashioned regional parliament. A joint council of guild representatives was to be made responsible for the efficient conduct of industry, but the consumer, through parliament, was to set the goals for production. Rates of pay and the total wage bill (to which the pricing of goods was to conform as closely as possible, since the ideal guild price-level, the "just price," was supposed to fluctuate around cost-of-production-and-sale) were to be set by the Joint Council and a committee of parliament, subject to revision at intervals. Each separate guild—the miners' guild, the transport workers' guild, the distributive guild, and so on—was to be a democratic, self-governing body, with local councils sending representatives to district councils, and district councils heading up in the national council. Guild membership was always to be open at the bottom, on the principle of first-come, first-served; if all the guilds were full-up the State would have to support the waiting neophytes. During periods of unemployment or sickness, guild members would continue to draw their pay. Expulsion from a guild was to be made extremely difficult, with an outside court making the ultimate decision. Grounds for expulsion were to be non-political, analogous, say, to the indulgence in unethical practices by a physician. The guilds were to control the "how" of their work—the hours, the tempos, the shop conditions. As to the apportionment of pay, each guild was to receive money in proportion to membership: same size guilds, same size pay. But division of pay within the guild was to be as each individual guild chose: if a guild wanted to reward its members on the share-and-share-alike basis it was free to do so. A guildsman was to be free to save, but his money would gather no interest. Trading, as contrasted with production, was to be under national control, with parliament determining price levels and wage levels and new investment through its control of the national purse. Foreign trading, a matter of barter, was to be a government monopoly. Ordinary private property—homes, pleasure automobiles, small land holdings, and petty industry of one type or another—was to be left undisturbed; the guildsmen took that much from Belloc's notion of the Distributive, as opposed to the Capitalist or Socialist, State. Socialist demands for the total obliteration of private property were dismissed as "pedantry"; after all, it was the type of property that was important, and the guildsmen were only trying to pull the claws of the plutocrats who were entrenched behind the legal device of the big corporation.

A grand and glorious picture. Whether it was a picture that contained fatal flaws just under the surface pigments, whether the whole doctrine is full of "bugs," we shall never really know. Guild socialist handling of the problem of investment seems quite vague: after all, money must be issued in the form of wages to cover the fabrication of capital goods, and if guildsmen were to decide to spend that money on consumers' goods instead of saving it at no interest an inflation would be bound to result. But, since the war, both communist and fascist governments have learned how to cancel money issued to create capital equipment that is non-purchasable by the common man; they do it by taxing back part of the total issued "purchasing power," or by forcing the people to buy government bonds. Thus the price level for consumers' goods is kept even. Given a guild socialist society, the monetary-investment problem would probably be solved through trial-and-error procedure, just as it was solved by Marxist society in Russia and by State-capitalist society in Germany.

So far as democracy is concerned, "vocational" representation may or may not be a snare and a delusion. Arthur Garfield Hays, in his recent "Democracy Works," argues that it is; in any event, he says, the pressure group insures sufficient vocational representation even under a parliamentary system that bases itself on regional elections. To Mr. Hays's way of thinking, the farm bloc, the beet sugar lobby and Labor's Non-Partisan League are the American substitute for a vocational parliament to balance the regional parliament.

Blocked Roads to Freedom

In Russia there was a brief experiment with vocational democracy, and many British guildsmen threw their caps in the air when Lenin proclaimed his slogan, "All power to the Soviets." But the "soviets" of workers and farmers were quickly put under the thumb of the Bolshevik Party, which arrogated to itself the "vocation of leadership" amid the confusions and alarums of the revolution. If the autonomy of the separate guilds were to be established by peaceful means fully covered by the amended law of the land, there is no reason to suppose that a single political party could seize full power in a guild society. A Bukharin, a Rykov, a Tomsky or a Trotsky presumably could find an economic base for political opposition by appealing to one set of guilds against another, or by fighting in parliament over regional aspects of economics (the location of roads, the draining of swamps, the use of Scottish ores as against the Welsh). Whether the establishment of the guild system would tend to choke off new industry is a more serious question: with the mechanism of the free market abolished in favor of a "market socialism," which is only an approximation of the real thing, there would be little incentive to experiment with, say, magnesium alloys at the expense of aluminum, or with plastics at the expense of steel. But even this might be solved by the maintenance of guild laboratories in conjunction with a flexible attitude toward the guilds themselves: the aluminum guild, for example, could be easily expanded to include the magnesium guild, insofar as the latter promised a better product at less expense.

Far more crucial than these "might be's" is the problem of getting from capitalist society to guild society. The English guildsmen used to talk about the method of "encroaching control" of industry, by which they meant the consolidation of union supervision over shop conditions under capitalist society. (The institution of the union-elected checkweighman at the mine head is an example of "encroaching control.") But nothing very much came of this theory of guild socialist "gradualism"; in all vital matters the capitalists held on to their "rights." During a London building trades lockout in 1914, the London Building Industries Federation made a contract with the Theosophical Society to put up a building, and the workers themselves assumed the responsibility for good work (although they refused financial responsibility). This elimination of the capitalist contractor was hailed by guildsmen as a notable advance; and after the war further experiments were made with guilds in the building trades. But guilds found it difficult to get a "collective contract," i.e., the disbursement of a lump sum to the guild itself for a job done, with payment to guild members portioned out as the guild itself voted. The capitalists insisted on keeping control of the wage structure in their own hands; hence the elimination of the middle-man in the building industry did not bring about a revolutionary change in the system of rewards.

Blocked Roads to Freedom

Since the great here-to-there problem remained incapable of practical solution as long as corporations had the same property rights as individuals, guildsmen gave up trying in the post-war years. It has become more and more apparent, since 1918, that little practical good can come of trying to create a blue-print-perfect society overnight; engineers of social change must work with institutions as they exist in the present, and the future can only grow out of the exceedingly imperfect past. Besides, the problem of keeping even a minimal amount of freedom alive in the face of fascist "encroaching control" has become so urgent that radicals everywhere must bend their energies to meeting more immediate problems than the constitution of a guild society. They must work to stimulate investment, to expand total production, and to raise the level of real wages within the given orbit of capitalism, lest a contracting economic system cry out overwhelmingly for the military rule that is necessary in a state of siege.

Nevertheless, something will come of Guild Socialism some day. Indeed, something has come of it already. For insofar as the Russians grant economic liberty to groups, they do it along guild lines, permitting the agricultural collectives to control the disposal of at least part of their produce. If Soviet Russia is ever to become a true democracy—i.e., if it is ever to become more Soviet than Russia—it will do it by extending the guild principle. As for the U. S., its heritage from the

I.W.W. industrial union movement continues to push it in a Guild Socialist direction. John L. Lewis's forceful but still somewhat inchoate demand for "industrial democracy" is, at bottom, a simple demand for the "encroaching control" of old Guild Socialist theory. And who knows? Maybe the C.I.O., in its quest for plant democracy, will rediscover in action the more vital principles of Guild Socialism. These principles will have to be supplemented by other principles if society as a whole is to be reconstituted along democratic lines. But a program does not have to be adopted in its entirety to have value; and the Guild Socialists may still have much to say even in a period of partial recrudescence of their aims and desires.

In the meantime the world rocks on; and growing points for Guild Socialism are few and far between. Old roads to freedom remain blocked; radical politics in the U. S. lacks even an effective political party of its own. We are constrained to makeshifts for the foreseeable future; and so turn to that *faute de mieux* organization for liberalism, the Democratic Party.

Whose Democratic Party?

WHEN Phil La Follette called a meeting of progressives to form a new political party—the National Progressives of America—at Madison, Wisconsin, in the Spring of 1938, he gestured into a social void. The "party of our time" failed utterly to click; free lance radicals were cool; Communists yelled Fascism; and Roosevelt men sourly remarked that Phil had no business rocking the New Deal boat. The Democratic Party, they said, would do very well.

Nevertheless, Phil La Follette spoke at the turn, not out of turn. For the New Deal ship, as a progressive ship, was already sinking from a hole in the bottom, not from any water taken in over the gunwales. Having sat at the feet of his very practical father, Phil La Follette was quite aware that American politics follow a number of rhythmic patterns, the proper understanding of which should enable any prescient person to make reasonably accurate forecasts. One of the reasonably certain patterns is that no President ever gets anything done during the last two years of his second term. Woodrow Wilson didn't; Theodore Roosevelt didn't. And it was a pretty safe bet when Phil La Follette spoke out that Franklin D. Roosevelt would,

75

barring the expected outbreak of the Second World War, spend his seventh and eighth years in the White House fighting a desperate rearguard action to save legislation that was already on the books.

There are *institutional* reasons for the sterility of a President's seventh and eighth years. For, by the time a second administration has passed its midpoint, a President, no matter how popular, ceases to have any coat-tails worth hanging to; the patronage which he can still hand out is generally of such poor quality and such short duration that it is hardly worth the taking.

To illustrate my point, let us look at the chief institutional check upon a President's second-term legislative demands: the United States Senate. The Senate is in every way an anomalous institution; in the tripartite division of the powers it acts as a check within a check. Viewed from a seat in the press gallery on any ordinary day, the Senate is a pretty undignified body: its members come and go in the filtered half-light like so many clubmen slouching about in their favorite reading room. Long-nosed Joe Bailey of North Carolina may be making a sober speech about the weakening of our moral fiber, or Borah of Idaho may be denouncing Britain's complicity in the Nazification of Europe. Yet, whether the topic is great or small, it is all one to the senators, who continue to sign their mail, gaze at the ceiling, or mumble casually to each other.

Once upon a time, when its members were chosen indirectly, by vote of the state legislatures, the Senate had the reputation of being a lordly body—the finest gentlemen's club in the world next to the British House of Lords. Since 1913 it has been directly responsible to the voters. But neither direct popular elections nor the ineffectual atmosphere of the Senate Chamber has any real bearing on the average senator's feeling of proud independence. A senator is not usually amenable to ordinary party discipline for more than two years out of the six of his official life; hence it is no accident that people like Daniel Webster, John C. Calhoun, Henry Clay, Old Bob La Follette and William Edgar Borah rate high in any list of incorrigible American individualists. Fearful of absolute democracy, the Founding Fathers provided for Senate independence not only by establishing the indirect method of selection but by fixing the term at six years and staggering the elections. Only a third of the Senate membership comes up for office at the two-year voting intervals. The practical upshot of the six-year term and the staggered elections is that two-thirds of the senators are under no absolute pressure from the White House during a President's second term.

To illustrate, let us look at the career of the lazy and witty Senator Pat Harrison of Mississippi. Pat "went along" with Roosevelt until 1936. But in that year, with the help of the President's coat-tails, he got himself re-elected for a term running until 1942. Working on the assumption that there would be no third term for his skipper, Pat felt perfectly safe in staging a mutiny. Presumably he will be beholden to a different chief in 1942. And the Senators who were re-elected in 1938—including the "unpurged" George of Georgia, Gillette of Iowa, Tydings of Maryland and Van Nuys of Indiana—felt doubly safe, for they don't come up for office again until 1944.

Even the Senators who come up for re-election in 1940 could afford to desert Roosevelt during his second term without fear of discipline from the titular party chief. For if the President does succeed in establishing his claim to a third term nomination, the 1940 class of senators will be in a position to trade in its opposition nuisance value for comfortable places on the band-wagon. It does not always pay political dividends to go down the line slavishly for the Big Boss; for when "disloyalty" is bought out, it sometimes commands more in terms of patronage than the "loyal" supporters get. Abstract loyalty has never been a political virtue; if one is to get ahead in politics, one must know when and where to threaten secession.

Since Phil La Follette knows a check-and-double-check-and-balance system when he sees one, he was on perfectly sound logical ground when he predicted, in the Spring of 1938, that the Democratic Party was through for the time being as a progressive party. Though the Supreme Court might be "liberalized" through Roosevelt appointees, Phil La Follette knew that the Senate could be counted on to take its place as democracy's curb bit. When a President loses his patronage power, the stagger system of senatorial election guarantees that the upper House shall split apart even when party loyalty to the chief executive is not the issue. For inasmuch as no two senators from a given state come in on the same ground swell of popular emotion, they tend to have antagonistic ideas even when they are members of the same party. Like competing prima donnas, they frequently hate each other even more than they hate the opposition. Let us take Pat Harrison for our example again. Pat is a civilized person; his Democratic colleague from Mississippi, Theodore "The Man" Bilbo, is a demagogue who nurses his grudges. At last reports neither was speaking to the other. So when Bilbo votes "yes," Pat says "no." A somewhat similar situation exists for Montana, which is represented by two Democratic senators, Burton K. Wheeler and James E. Murray. Provoked because Murray got some patronage which, theoretically, should have gone to the senior senator, Wheeler's opposition to the "regular" party will as expressed by Murray has been intensified. When you add personal intra-House antagonisms to the immunity from presidential reprisal, you get an institutional check in the Senate that goes way beyond the power of the Supreme Court to negate the popular will as it was expressed by Roosevelt's 1936 majority.

But Phil La Follette had further logic on his side in 1938. To begin with, the Democratic Party can only function for liberalism when it has a strong nationally-minded leader. Roosevelt has been just such a leader. But men of his caliber are usually followed by weak men. Unable to pick a strong crown prince who would please the organization Democrats down the line, Roosevelt was on the spot even as early as 1938. He could, of course, try to run again himself in 1940. But, as we shall see, this brings up all sorts of knotty problems, some of which are practically insoluble for a President who wishes to remain a force for progressivism. And assuming that Roosevelt is through in 1940, the past history of the Democratic Party offers no real assurance for liberals.

From the very start the Democratic Party has been the despair or the laughingstock of people who make consistency their test of politics. Founding Father Thomas Jefferson, with his disrelish for the human products of city life, originally created the party to serve as an exponent of the political purity of west county Virginia, a land of small freehold farmers. Yet this pure corn-fed organization almost immediately drew the support of venal power-hunters from New York State who stood ready as brokers to buy and sell the votes of the urban slums. The Tammany Society of New York, political property of the raffish Aaron Burr, was part of the Democratic Party almost from the beginning. And the ancient paradox still persists: the party is today a loose federation of southern cotton snobs, western dirt farmers (the real heirs of Jefferson), and the machines of Jersey City's Frank Hague, Chicago's Pat Nash and Ed Kelly, the Irish bosses of Boston, and so on.

Besides inconsistencies of personnel, the Democratic Party exhibits philosophical inconsistencies which are the subject of scorn on the part of people who are fond of invoking debaters' tricks. It is supposedly the party of "states' rights." Yet Grover Cleveland and Woodrow Wilson were federalists when it was a matter of breaking the Pullman Strike in Illinois or using "force to the utmost, force without stint or limit," in a great foreign war. The Democratic Party is allegedly equalitarian. Yet in the Deep South it has stood ever since 1840 for the racial supremacy of the white man.

These are easy ironies to note. But, as Herbert Agar has recently pointed out, it is important to distinguish between Jefferson's ends and Jefferson's means. Jefferson himself did not pause very long over the abstraction of States' Rights or strict construction of the Constitution when he had the chance to buy the Louisiana Territory for a prayer and a song. And his unpopular embargo of 1807 was a federal act which denied in practice the "right" of the New England states to ship goods as they pleased to the warring nations of Napoleonic Europe.

If we follow Herbert Agar and assert that Jefferson's end, as proclaimed in the Declaration of Independence, was "equal rights for all, special privileges for none," then the Jeffersonian means fall into place as contributory only when conditions are favorable to their success. The means to the Jeffersonian end, in the society of the early nineteenth century, was decentralization of political power. But Jefferson lived in a time of decentralized economic power, and he was certain that federal authority would be used, not to promote equality, but to strengthen economic privilege that would effectively deny equality. After all, he was fighting Federalist Alexander Hamilton, who considered the people a Great Beast.

Events have, of course, played hob with the Jeffersonian end and the Jeffersonian means and conditions. During the generation that followed the Jacksonian epoch, the Democratic Party fell under the enchanter's spell of John C. Calhoun and the theorists of a "Greek democracy" of free citizens resting on the backs of slaves. Calhoun was Jeffersonian in his insistence on States' Rights. But he used the Jeffersonian means in order to aggrandize the power of the cotton snobs and to deny "equal rights" to the Negro. The means had, as is so often the case, become the end. It took the Republican Party under Lincoln to make the Jeffersonian end even partially available to the black man—and the means of Lincoln were, of course, a Hamiltonian denial of States' Rights. After the Civil War was over, the growth of the giant corporation compounded the irony of events by wiping out the conditions deemed necessary to the functioning of the Jeffersonian means and the attainment of the Jeffersonian end.

Whose Democratic Party?

So the modern Jeffersonian is faced with a dilemma. If he refuses to invoke federal political power he can hardly hope to disturb the centralized economic power that is making Jeffersonian equality a vain dream. The means of States' Rights are no longer effective to Jefferson's end, which is why the prattling about them comes today from conservatives who have more or less cornered the means and materials of production and are withholding them from the common run of humanity. If the modern Jeffersonian is a gallant and fighting soul such as Franklin D. Roosevelt, he will decide to take the chance with centralized political power as an offset to the centralized economic power of the "interests," or the "200 corporations," or Mr. Lundberg's "sixty families," or the "money power," or whatever. He may be building a Frankenstein power-mechanism that will, eventually, create its own autocratic and non-Jeffersonian end. But if he doesn't choose to run the risk he loses the battle at the outset.

Such being the case, the correct Jeffersonian test to apply to the present-day institution of Mr. Roosevelt's party is a subtle one. Faced with the phenomenon of Soil Conservation, or WPA, or housing loans, one must ask: "Is the Party invoking the central power in order to create economic conditions that will eventually enable it to relinquish that power?" If it is, then it is acting in a Jeffersonian way. But because a party is not only the embodiment of a set of ideas but an institution that is also interested in salaries, perquisites, kudos and the

83

thrill that one gets from exercising power, the *institutional* aspirations of Rooseveltians must be continually watched. It is not true that Harry Hopkins ever prostituted the WPA for election purposes; that job was done —where it was done, as in Pennsylvania and Kentucky —by local bigwigs and satraps. But the American people showed they were aware of the correct Jeffersonian test when they raised the issue of the politicalization of relief. A party must never be permitted to let its institutional needs get the better of its social ideas.

As successful parties go, the party of Mr. Roosevelt has been pretty well behaved; the Hopkinses, the Wallaces, the Ickeses, have not subordinated their exalted Jeffersonian aims to more mundane institutional urges. Some of the New Deal legislation will seem permanently good; and Roosevelt has certainly established a social service base-line which no *non-fascist* party will ever dare remove. The New Deal's major methods of surmounting crisis, however, have not been *Jeffersonianly* correct for any long pull. They have not been pitched directly at increasing the long-term social power —i.e., the continuing ability to get at the means and materials of production—of the average individual. AAA and Soil Conservation have merely preserved the status quo of the more fortunate farmers and have actually worked to impoverish tenants and share-croppers. The Wagner Act and the National Labor Relations Board have certainly helped labor in its power to organize. But they have not demonstrably helped to create continuity and volume of employment, with the Jeffersonian corollary of a chance to store up small individual capital. And the WPA, however much it has added to the beauty and fundamental wealth of America, is only a stop-gap. It does not rehabilitate Americans as *producers* with a stake in the materials of production and the capital equipment of the country.

None of this is offered in criticism of Soil Conservation, the Wagner Act, or the WPA. They have all been necessary, and they will remain necessary for a long time, even under a Republican regime. The Rooseveltians are not to be condemned for spending their major energies on fighting fire with whatever hoses came to hand. Crop limitation, WPA and NLRB all come under the head of fire fighting and are essential in the sense that people must first of all be kept alive if they are even to aspire to the Jeffersonian end at some future date.

But the point which the student of history must make is that no political party can stay in office forever by using the same old makeshifts. There must be new construction as well as jobs for the fire patrol. Once the tricks of fire-fighting have been learned, any party can serve as Engine Company No. 1; the Tories have proved that to the liberals and laborites of England. But the party which aspires to shape the long-term future of the U. S. must devote more and more of its energies to devising ways and means of getting the unemployed off WPA and into productive activity in private and decentralized public corporation business. And the party of the future must be thinking of ways of rewarding farmers not for producing less of what they are producing now, but for producing more of the things that can be sold locally, without regard to Liverpool international prices. Concretely, the AAA of the future will result in more cabbages and soybeans and less cotton, not merely in less cotton.

Most of the so-called "constructive" criticism of the Democratic Party has come from people who merely pretend to have Jeffersonian interests at heart. Even those who talk loud and long about decentralizing economic power as a step toward decentralizing political control are unwilling to get out and work for the consumer co-operative movement, or for the fostering of a large class of small debt-free farmers, or for a practical solution of the monopoly question as it applies to access to the means of production. Hence, in filing my own particular demurrer, I don't wish to be put down as an anti-Rooseveltian. The virtue of Mr. Roosevelt as a party leader is that for six years he did a magnificent job of fire-fighting without disastrously alienating any of the Democratic power groups with which a Democratic Party politician must work. In doing this job, Mr. Roosevelt has certainly not closed the door on a democratic, Jeffersonian solution of the problem of economic centralism. If and when he is elected, the next Democratic president will still have the opportunity to carry the country back at least a short distance toward the Jeffersonian ideal—which is not to say that a Democrat will be elected in 1940, or that he will necessarily use his opportunity if elected.

It has become the fashion to speak of Democratic Party economic legislation as a jumble of cross-purposes; and it is true that crop limitation is hardly the way to the more abundant life. But politics is the art of one-thing-at-a-time: if an AAA means tragedy for the share-cropper who is thrown off the land by cotton control, then the politician will get around to the share-cropper—*next*. As a matter of fact, there has been a deep natural consistency, as contrasted with verbal consistency, to the regional and group coalition that put Roosevelt into office in 1932 and 1936. Had someone of the intellectual perceptions of a de Tocqueville or a Bryce visited this country in 1931 he would not have predicted Revolution—as did so many of the native seers—but a New Deal very like the one we have had. Analyzing the disaffected power-groupings of that year, he would have summed them up as five in number— five legs to the amazing 1931 Democratic donkey. The first leg would have been the plexus of interests that try to make a living out of the primary commodity of cotton; the second leg would have been the similar grouping that lives off corn, hogs and wheat. A third leg would have been city labor—as Frank Murphy so well understood when he sat in the Detroit City Hall and listened to the angry murmurs of ex-River Rouge em-

ployees in the streets outside. The fourth leg could only
have been discerned by someone who took the trouble
to visit California and the Pacific Northwest, where old
people from "back East" in Io-way and Kansas revived
the emotional grievances of Populism and Bryanism the
moment their pitiful retirement income disappeared in
the wake of the crash. And the fifth leg, suddenly
sprouting from the Democratic donkey as an anatomical
miracle, would have been the liberals and ideologues of
various shades. This group of people was not important
numerically but very significant as intellectual leaven.
Inasmuch as the liberal intellectuals had been the only
ones to busy themselves with "planning" during the fat
Twenties, they had a natural advantage of position
when "practical" politicians came seeking ideas.

The coalition of five elements did not constitute a
homogeneous class party. But it did constitute a grouping that had a common immediate enemy: the workings
of a financial system that was keeping them from access
to the materials of production. Since one common denominator, one solvent, one strong non-divisive interest, is as good as another in politics, despite the teach-
ings of the Marxists, this was sufficient unto the day for
Franklin D. Roosevelt.

As the 1940 convention approaches, the same common denominator will hold four of the five elements of
the coalition; only the strange fifth leg of the animal,
the group of liberal intellectuals, will be trying to walk
away from the rest. The southern Democrats must still

88

look after cotton, the western Democrats after corn and wheat. The northern city machines, fetid though they may be in most respects, must still play ball with the C.I.O. *or* the A. F. of L., and the old folks of California and the Pacific Northwest will still be found backing any one of fifty-seven varieties of the Townsend Plan. With these realities in mind, one can safely predict a party platform that advocates continuation of benefit payments to agriculture, a labor relations act (perhaps modified because labor itself is badly split), and some form of relief and old-age security. As a matter of fact, the New Deal base line will be accepted in *both* party platforms.

But this is not to say that the Democrats will back a fighting Roosevelt, or a fighting Roosevelt man—or that Roosevelt himself will not succumb to the lure of compromise. For two things have changed since 1932 and 1936: the Republicans have, in some states, started to outbid the Democrats as champions of the old folks (they may be demagogic about it, but a demagogue's vote counts the same as any other); and the liberal intellectuals have ceased to regard the original New Deal as anywhere near enough. Conservative candidates will be quite as ready as liberal candidates with promises of *necessary* spending; hence the radicals won't be able to capitalize all the Santa Claus appeal. And the liberal intellectuals, insisting on a solution of the monopoly problem, on a comprehensive housing program, on health insurance, on an extension of the TVA principle, on an adventurous new tax program, will be so far out of touch with all the numerically strong power groups that they can have little effect on the convention choice.

Rather than curtail spending for relief, the liberal intellectuals have been fighting to increase it—with the benefits coming from Mr. Roosevelt's own hand. They are aware that pump priming has failed, but the idea of "leverage" spending—i.e., of government lending and government-underwritten investment to stimulate the capital goods market, which, in turn, would result in consumer spending as wages are paid out—has gained many adherents among the Left Wing coterie. The liberal intellectuals are certain that the capitalist system cannot run any longer under its own steam; and if there is to be no artificial stimulation they want to pin the blame for depression on the old-line Democrats and the Republicans. They want, in brief, to be in a position to say, "I told you so." Unfortunately, depression between now and 1941 will be blamed on the Roosevelt administration no matter how many successful coalitions are organized in Congress to defeat Rooseveltian leverage spending. The White House occupant is always left holding the bag in bad or uncertain times.

I happen to think the liberal intellectuals are right about the inability of the capitalist system to run by itself unless extensive alterations are first made. With State-protected debt tokens running far beyond the ability of capital equipment to earn interest and amortization charges, new investment cannot happen of its own

90

free will, or under the "invisible hand" of Adam
Smith's God. But belief is not power; and all the liberal
intellectuals have at the moment is their belief. Alfred
Bingham senses a new spirit of dedication among the
New Dealers, who are just now coming to realize that
John Maynard Keynes's proposed "socialization of investment" may be a free people's substitute for socialism. But this belated dedication comes too late for 1940;
it will have to be held in reserve for 1944. The right-
ist and middle-of-the-road Democrats have something
more tangible than a spirit of dedication; they have
the balance-of-power in Congress. Having accepted the
1932-38 New Deal base line *as the new conservatism*,
they can more or less stand pat on existing social legislation and proceed to gun for the President and his liberal intellectual allies. The 1938 elections, which were
so spotty, offer them plenty of excuse, if not a "mandate," for such tactics. No one knows what will happen
in the few months that lie between us and the nominating convention, but the conservative Democrats are
pretty sure they can keep a liberal intellectual New
Dealer of the stripe of Robert Jackson or Harry Hopkins from becoming either candidate or President. The
spread of the European War may confuse all issues,
but the conservatives of the Democratic Party are count-
ing on wangling the situation—and maybe Mr. Roosevelt, through the offices of Mr. Farley—their way even
amid the alarums of neutrality fights. What funds are
appropriated for politicalized spending in this final pre-

convention session of Congress will certainly be earmarked in such a way that Roosevelt will get no credit
for them; both the conservative Democrats and the
Townsendized Republicans will want to take the credit
for any last-minute largesse themselves.

The trouble with the liberal intellectuals in the
New Deal is that they reckoned without the South.
They knew that South Carolina and Arkansas and Texas
were safely Democratic; they knew that Joe Robinson
and Jimmy Byrnes and Cactus Jack Garner were "party
men." Consequently, they counted on winning the day
for the President's progressive program without ever
having to bother with anything below the Mason-Dixon
line. That section, so they argued, was "in the bag." It
couldn't go Republican, so it must go New Deal.

For one term the liberal intellectuals looked right;
Joe Robinson, as Democratic Senate majority leader,
"went along" against all his conservative instincts, and
even the irascible Carter Glass compromised his supposedly fourteen-carat intransigence in 1936 on election
day when it was a question of saving his own political
hide. But, as we have seen, a second term is never like a
first; as soon as the pre-election hoop-la was over in
1936 the "party men" began to think in terms of a future, not the present, President. With the inevitable second-term revival of party uncertainty, the "party men"
became even less interested in a united front than the
few liberal Mugwumps. Hence the post-1936 revolt of

practically the entire South, that region of "party men," from the rule of the liberal intellectuals of the New Deal.

The American South of 1939 is a curious combination, one which a Rhode Island liberal such as Tommy Corcoran, or a New York-Iowa liberal such as Harry Hopkins, will almost certainly fail to beat with the northern wing of the Democratic Party. On the one hand the American South is flagrantly reactionary—a land of tobacco-drooling post-Confederate tradition in which politicians can still cadge crucial votes in the Democratic primaries by threatening to crucify the Pope and to burn uppity niggers. This is the South of the bitter Representative Gene Cox of Georgia, of South Carolina's antediluvian Cotton Ed Smith. As Maury Maverick put it, all progressive social legislation founders in the reactionary South on one attitude—the attitude of: "Jeezus Chris', you ain't goin' to pay no nigger sixteen bucks a week, are you?" The rhetorical question answers itself; it means an end to southern co-operation on progressive bills.

There is, however, another South—the South of old-fashioned Manchester free-trade liberalism. This South is typified by the persistence of Secretary of State Cordell Hull, whose economics—in its more unchastened aspects—dates back to Grover Cleveland's day. In terms of theory, this liberalism is sufficient, but it counts on a world spirit of international co-operation for the extension of free trade that will not see a recrudescence in

93

our generation. In terms of what Dixie needs (primarily the salvaging of some of her overseas cotton markets) Manchester liberalism is still progressive; in terms of what the nation must inexorably face as a whole in this day of continental regionalism it is nineteenth century and reactionary. And the North cannot permanently like it, for it looks to the decay or the displacement of northern manufacturing areas, and to an end to the predominantly east-west movement of American trade. In order that a natural shift may take place the Southerners want no new laws that will interfere with the normal higgling of a free-variable market. To the Manchesterian South, equalizing wage-and-hour legislation, for example, means the destruction of a natural advantage. For the South can support its labor power more cheaply than the North for the simple reason that it has no large fuel bills to pay. Its ruling groups want to take advantage of the benefits of nature for the next generation, at least.

For investment purposes, the American South is one of the few remaining lands of free capitalist promise. Its acres of slash and loblolly pine can be easily turned into paper; its textile mill sites are much closer to sources of raw material supply than the old mills of Rhode Island and northeastern Connecticut. The South has not yet become the furniture maker for the United States, but go to Grand Rapids, Michigan, and listen to the complaints about cheap southern stuff and cheap southern workers if you want to know what the South can do in this line. The South is the home of the gulf oil and the gulf sulphur belts; it is rapidly becoming a center of chemical and fertilizer industries. Even Pittsburgh and Ohio and Chicago may be threatened as steel centers by Alabama. For, unlike Pennsylvania and Ohio, the Birmingham region can obtain its iron ore, its coal and its limestone—the essentials for steel—from within one small local compass. The Birmingham deposits are, of course, owned by northern capital that is also invested in Pittsburgh, but that will not prove an insuperable obstacle when growing southern industrialism wants metal.

It is perfectly true that this remaining land of capitalist promise hasn't any native capital to speak of. And it is true that the dividends it now produces have a habit of vanishing into New York, as Professor Walter Prescott Webb has so eloquently proved in his "Divided We Stand." But the South, like any colonial preserve, has a class that makes its living by doing local managerial and legal work for absentee interests, and this class gets the bulk of the effective southern representation in Congress. Again as Maury Maverick says, this class is, from a functional standpoint, the ablest in the South. In one sense it is more Wall Street than Tom Lamont, but it is also loyal to the South in a way that any growing native middle class is loyal to its homeland. Like an enterprising South African or Australian who borrows from London, the Georgian who depends on New York for his financing or his salary or his fees does so in hopes of gathering enough gear to cut free from the outland in the future.

With the need for capital ever present in his mind, a certain type of Saving Southerner in Congress is naturally bound to the Manchester version of liberalism. This type of southern representative symbolizes a natural sectional culture-lag, and it is no very queer phenomenon that the most vociferous budget-balancers of Mr. Roosevelt's party come from Virginia, the Carolinas and Mississippi. A man like Senator Bailey of North Carolina grew up in a wasted Confederate land; he remembers a childhood spent saving apple cores to feed to the chickens. Now that industry is slowly inching southward, Joe Bailey doesn't want to see free capitalism give way to an American allotrope of State Socialism before he and his kind have tasted the sweets which England, Holland and the American northeast have already gorged upon.

Hence the importance of Joe Bailey and of Virginia's Harry Byrd, of Cactus Jack Garner and Pat Harrison, of Jesse Jones of Texas and Bernard M. Baruch of South Carolina, to any consideration of the future performance of the Democratic Party. Working shrewdly behind the scenes to save the "traditional" Democracy of Grover Cleveland from the latter-day Bryanism of Franklin D. Roosevelt, these men have freely combined with northern Democratic conservatives such as Ed Burke of Nebraska and Gerry of Rhode Island to chisel down the demands of the northern liberal intel-

lectuals. Almost certainly they will hold enough power
to nominate a compromise New Deal candidate in 1940.
They may get fooled if they compromise on some obscure Democratic governor who is a sleeping Roosevelt
liberal. But in that case, the behind-the-scenes combinations and deals will commence all over again once the
new President has exhausted his patronage.

In the Summer of 1938, after suffering humiliating
defeats on the Supreme Court and reorganization bill
issues, the liberal intellectuals suddenly realized that
the Democratic Party as constituted was not sufficient to
their purposes. Only a party with a national leader bent
on following the gleam, only a strong federal organization capable of handling both the Cotton Ed Smiths and
the Joe Baileys of the South and the local bosses of the
northern cities, was equal to their demands. They had
the leader. But the opportunity of creating a strong federal organization, of getting continuous popular support for a Roosevelt program, was slipping fast. How
to reverse the trend? How to force the supposed 1936
mandate of the people on the Saving Southerners and
the local bosses? The answer, hastily conceived, was the
"purge."

A lot of nonsense has been printed about the "im-
morality" of the purge. The conservatives—who certainly know a thing or two about enforcing "regularity"
themselves—have muttered things about supposedly
comparable events in Germany and in Russia. They

have painted the so-called "elimination committee" of Mr. Corcoran in colors only applicable to the Ogpu or the Gestapo of a one-party State. Actually, a party purge cannot be undemocratic in a two-or-multiple-party country. For a purge must be carried out democratically, by vote; and a purged party functionary can always join the opposition or seek to start a new party of his own. He is not deprived of opportunity to earn a livelihood or shut up in a concentration camp, as in a one-party State. He even has the right to purge the purgers and eliminate the elimination committee—if he can get the party majority on his side.

If Tommy Corcoran had sought historical justification for the attempted 1938 purge he could easily have found it. For in the post-Jacksonian times John C. Calhoun of South Carolina, who had only recently returned to the Democratic Party after a period of dalliance in the ranks of the Whigs, decided to purge the southern party organizations of all Jeffersonian equalitarian influence. Calhoun eventually succeeded in his ambitious program, with the result that Calhoun Democrats control most of the southern state organizations to this day. Had the "elimination" committee wished to take high historical ground it could have insisted that it was merely trying to drive the Calhoun-cuckoos out of the usurped Jeffersonian nest. It could have gone to war under a slogan of "Out with the Whigs!"

Such justification, of course, would not have been practical politics in a South still suffering from Civil

Whose Democratic Party?

War hangovers and still responsive to the magic of Calhoun's name. The purge campaign had to proceed under paler and safer auspices, as a battle between "liberalism" and "reaction." But since the South doesn't understand post-Manchester progressivism, the slogans used by the elimination committee didn't mean very much to the followers of Georgia's Senator George.

If the Democratic Party actually stands for the Jeffersonian end of "Equal Rights for All, Special Privileges for None," then Roosevelt had a perfect right to his purge. For he was merely trying to swing the party back to Jeffersonian tenets and away from the Calhoun heresy. In England, where the party leaders work out party platforms and the whips force them through even in the face of partial party opposition, Tommy Corcoran's notion of democratic discipline would seem obviously intelligent. And the Corcoran tactics ought not to be misunderstood in the U. S. For under the American system the only way party discipline can be enforced is by methods not contemplated in the dreams of the Founding Fathers.

Our Founding Fathers mistook the English system for one of complete check-and-balance separation of the powers, and they forthwith made their historical mistake the basis of the American system. As a result, our President is legally a mere rubber stamp, charged with carrying out the legislative mandate of Congress. If a President stands on the letter of the law he reduces himself to the role of traffic cop combined with the job of reporter-to-Congress-on-the-state-of-the-nation. But the American people don't actually approve of presidential rubber stamps, as the homage they pay to Washington, Jefferson, Jackson, Lincoln, Cleveland, Theodore Roosevelt and Wilson proves. Actually, they expect their President to be a party leader, at least to some extent. They expect him to assume the dual role of the British Prime Minister, who acts in both a legislative and executive capacity (with no veto by the judiciary). The American people do not believe in strict construction of the doctrine which says the powers of legislature, executive and judiciary shall be entirely separated.

If our system is not to bog down into a state of chronic civil war between the separated powers, some extra-legal co-ordination is necessary. Roosevelt sought to get his extra-legal co-ordination, first, by putting Congressional pincers on a recalcitrant Supreme Court, and, second, by getting his own men elected to Congress. As to the wisdom of the particular court plan which Roosevelt chose, there is much room for argument, as we shall see; many who "went along" with him on the plan privately considered it a stupid maneuver. But as to the President's right to a court plan (legally submitted to Congress) and a purge attempt (legally carried out in the primaries) there can be no logical or moral objection. It is true that a President can use his patronage powers in a way calculated to negate the will of the majority which is asked to vote for a court plan or a purge. But this is part of the pathology of democratic procedure, and it doesn't alter the fundamental democratic need for party discipline. If the citizens object to a purge, it is their duty to see to it that patronage does not affect democratic choice of candidates; there is no check on the misuse of the patronage "muscle" except popular awareness and popular honesty.

The trouble with the Corcoran-directed purge of 1938, then, was not that it was "immoral" or "undignified." The trouble with it was that it was poorly planned and badly timed. It probably grew up like a mushroom (and with all a mushroom's lack of anchorage in the soil) out of a feeling of confidence inspired by the early 1938 New Deal primary victories of Senator Pepper in Florida and Senator Hill in Alabama. But these victories were delusive; in Florida a repeal of the old poll tax law had effectively spread the suffrage, while in Alabama, a relatively advanced southern industrial state, labor organizations had helped pay the poll taxes for their poorer members. In other southern states the same conditions did not pertain, and now that hindsight gives us a clear basis for criticism it can be argued that the liberal intellectuals should first have concentrated their efforts on forcing a change in the election laws that weight things in favor of the well-to-do in Georgia, South Carolina, Texas, Virginia, Tennessee and Mississippi. In most of these states the Rooseveltians tried to purge the Calhoun-cuckoos, but, with 5,000,000 Dixie Negroes of voting age disfranchised and with poor whites unable to pay the poll taxes, the conclusion could only have been one thing: defeat. And it was defeat that the purgers met.

So the liberal intellectuals are to be blamed for forcing an issue either too soon or too late. They are not, however, to be blamed overmuch, for in politics nothing is certain. Regardless of the outcome, it is just as well that the purge was tried. For it gave dramatic proof of Phil La Follette's contention that the Democratic Party is essentially non-maneuverable beyond a certain point for progressive purposes.

The failure of the "elimination committee" to eliminate anyone of importance should serve to demonstrate that Democratic cohesion for national social legislation can only be had during the first term of a genuinely popular leader. Once it is apparent that a great popular Democratic personality is not going to run again for office, the party will almost certainly revert to type. It must fall back into the hands of the Garners and the Harrisons in the South, and into the laps of local bosses in the North. It must become again what it has been all along in history: a loose federation of agrarians and city labor led by politicians who have little in common with each other save an itching desire for jobs. In first terms under great Presidents, the Democratic Party can be welded and driven forward by idealism. In second terms the gleam dies, and the politicians take to wandering on a plateau.

If Phil La Follette was guilty of rocking the boat at

Whose Democratic Party?

Madison in the Spring of 1938, it was, in any long-term reckoning, a most gentle and forgivable sin. Progressives cannot afford to put their eternal trust in a party doomed to run on two cylinders most of the time. There is, however, one question that must be settled as to the immediate short-run uses of the Democratic Party, and that question involves Mr. Roosevelt's chances for a third term. Can the Master Political Broker of our generation get away with four more years? And would they be effective? Or, lacking a chance himself, can he use his immense authority to clear the way for La Guardia, or Bill Douglas, or one of the La Follette brothers—or even himself—on a third party ticket for 1944? Or will his prestige result in the candidacy of an unknown quantity, such as the office-hungry Paul McNutt? Or will he give in to his enemy, Burton Wheeler, who would make a good middle-of-the-road semi-liberal candidate? The very fact that these questions must be asked proves that Mr. Roosevelt is one of our most colorful chameleons. But chameleons can travel towards an objective, even while changing color. Let us look, therefore, at Mr. Roosevelt on his travels.

Two Master Brokers

CARL SANDBURG has written a great biography of a nation in travail, "Abraham Lincoln: The War Years," by the simple device of taking as his unifying thread the history of Mr. Lincoln's reputation. Some day a poet-historian will describe America of the fretful Thirties—and describe it fully and adequately—by writing a similar history of Mr. Roosevelt's reputation.

Eight years have now passed since Walter Lippmann, echoing an uninformed prejudice, spoke of Franklin D. Roosevelt as "a highly impressionable person without a firm grasp of public affairs and without very strong convictions . . . an amiable man with many philanthropic impulses, but he is not the dangerous enemy of anything. He is too eager to please." Since 1932 the "amiable" man, "eager to please," has outraged practically every organized pressure group in the U. S. The Chamber of Commerce and the National Association of Manufacturers have hated him. John L. Lewis has thought of him as a Judas. Farmers in Wisconsin and Minnesota have complained that Soil Conservation isn't enough. Democrats and Republicans have objected strenuously to *specific* items of Cordell Hull's reciprocal trade program. Peace groups have seen in him the Number One war-monger of the century. The curious thing about this animosity, however, is that it has never been concentrated in any one period of time: when the peace groups are hating Roosevelt, Wall Street bankers let up.

Meanwhile the President has retained the friendship and the confidence of vast masses of the population, as every *Fortune* and Gallup poll demonstrates. A majority of the people distrusts his advisers and sees in every move of the Corcoran-Cohen team a sinister plot to undermine the Republic. Yet the President stands by his hated advisers—and the people, paradoxically, admire him for it.

No historian interested in the role of the so-called "sixty families" in the U. S. can afford to overlook the story of Roosevelt's reputation: from the first pathetic grasping at NRA straws to the caddish vituperation of Liberty League days, from the crocodile-tear shock at the judicial appointment of Hugo Black (who had long since repented his Klannishness) to the frenzied assault on the harmless windmill of the reorganization bill, the history of Plutocrat's Progress through the Vale of the Thirties can be traced by reference to Mr. Roosevelt. The tergiversations of the Left can be similarly charted. In the days of NRA, before Popular Frontism became the spavined Trojan horse of the Communists and their Fellow Travelers, the *New Masses* cartooned Roosevelt as a putty-jawed forcible-feeble Social Fascist. Norman Thomas went about complaining that the New Deal had swiped good socialist oak planks only to

use them for the construction of a crazy lean-to. Books
and articles were written about the "gay reformer";
Mauritz Hallgren, for example, devoted an entire volume to proving that FDR was the agent of a *rentier*
class that was determined to live off productive labor
and enterprising capital alike. Later on the viewpoint of
the Left changed abruptly: Roosevelt was the radical's
white hope from 1936 to mid-1939. Now the Communists are deserting him again; and Fellow Travelers
who are deserting Stalin are also worried about the
New Deal foreign policy. When some Sandburg of the
future mines the contemporary periodical literature and
the headlines of the Thirties, a history of American attitudes toward types of social change will emerge clearly
from the opinions about Mr. Roosevelt.

All of which means that Franklin Delano Roosevelt's
place in history is assured; as Marquis Childs has said,
he will stand as a symbolic figure at the end of one era
and the beginning of another.

For myself, I must admit that I was just as mistaken
about Roosevelt in 1932 as Walter Lippmann or Hey-
wood Broun. I had been studying the history of American "reform" movements since the Eighteen-seventies,
and had yet to discover a "progressive" President who
had held to a reformer's line. Theodore Roosevelt had
tried it in the gr-r-and and glor-r-ious pre-war trust-
busting days, but the "banker's" panic of 1907 had
scared Franklin Delano's fifth cousin into presenting
United States Steel with the property of the shaky Ten-

nessee Coal and Iron Company, which was just what Judge Gary and J. P. Morgan wanted. Woodrow Wilson had made a brave beginning, but his domestic program drowned in the war which his finagling cabinet minister, Robert Lansing, did so much to foist upon us. Grover Cleveland had denounced the "communism of pelf"—what a subtler generation would call "big business collectivism"—but Cleveland's mild efforts to take inflated profits from the "communist"-industrialist's pockets by lowering the tariff came to very little in Congress. In the states west of the Mississippi the great "progressive" measures of the initiative, the referendum and the recall had produced very little: as Richard Neuberger complains, the initiative—or popular initiation of legislation by petition—has mostly been used to get "ham-and-eggs-every-Thursday" on the ballot or to increase the Oregon bounty on jack rabbits and sage rats. And in the cities—New York, Cleveland, Toledo, Chicago—"reform" mayors have been followed with distressing regularity by resurgent Tammany Halls.

History is supposed to be a great teacher, but unfortunately no statistician has shown us how to "weight" it. Lacking a proper weighting technique, the critics who had read and pondered the history of reform in America were not so far-sighted, so prescient or so lucky as Franklin D. Roosevelt. What the critics failed to see was that the balance of class and group forces had shifted greatly since 1912. In the old days "reform" could win whenever the Better Element was for it. But as soon as Nice People discovered that reform was touching them in the pocketbook they backslid into reactionary ways. They have been backsliding all through the New Deal second term, as an oblique reading of most newspaper editorial pages can tell you. The critics of the reformer in Roosevelt accurately foretold this fall-away. But they failed utterly to see that Nice People no longer hold the balance of power. That balance now rests with the groups that know they have nothing to gain in the pocketbook if reform dies. These groups can make mistakes—they may have made one in allowing Roosevelt to focus his attention on Europe. But they can win victories: the Better Element was against Senator Lister Hill in Alabama and Senator Pepper in Florida in 1938, yet Hill and Pepper came through, thanks to a circumvention and relaxation of the ancient poll tax requirements in their respective bailiwicks. In the North, where a good many Republican governors won in 1938, the New Deal fall-away was not due to a Better Element shift. It was due to a feeling of tiredness and disappointment among the poorer balance-of-power groups.

No matter what happens to Roosevelt in the future, history will record that he *felt* his way by sometimes-blind instinct toward good goals until the European war and the election of 1940 knocked him off his base. John T. Flynn, the President's most virulent liberal critic, is chary of giving him any credit at all. But Mr. Flynn, who has a clearly articulated economic philosophy, is not sufficiently appreciative of *political* difficulties and necessities. It is true that the wages-and-hours law, which Mr. Flynn admits is good, was only passed after five years of wrangling when, as Mr. Flynn says, the substance of it might have been had in 1933 with passage of an amended Black-Connery Thirty-hour bill. But NRA, the ill-fated Blue Eagle, had to be given its trial flight first. Our liberals, for better or worse, had been so impressed by Russian Five-year planning that failure to make the NRA experiment would have left many American social thinkers still hankering for a totally planned, as against a much more mobile and free *partially* planned, system. NRA was a movement toward slavery, toward a type of Chamber-of-Commerce Guild Fascism, but it was luckily tried out and exposed as a failure at a time when it could not kill us. We can count the NRA period as significant social insurance against any future revival of economic rule by the employers' trade associations.

Other measures which the President has pushed are more worthy of his pertinacity. As I have indicated, Soil Conservation and WPA have been necessary stop-gap measures. Whatever the shortcomings of Social Security, the principle is here to stay. The National Labor Relations Board may have its share of unwashed dirty linen hidden in the hamper, but it, too, represents something which we must have if labor is to have a *de facto* as well as a *de jure* bargaining power. SEC, which grew out of the Pecora investigation of the seamy side of

Wall Street, merely tries to enforce an Old Testament conception of common honesty: it will hardly disappear, although it may be laxly used by future administrations with a tender heart for the investment bankers. The Utility Holding Company Act is good as the SEC is good: it aims to prevent the fleecing of investors and consumers. As for TVA, it may be prostituted by the next Warren Gamaliel Harding to attain unto the White House, but the big dams built by the New Deal —in Oregon, Washington and Texas as well as in Tennessee—will be used and blessed by future generations.

History will record that Franklin Delano Roosevelt was a fighter. Sometimes he has fought badly. His 1938 purge was too hasty. He has frequently muffed chances by a failure to take his Congressional leaders into his confidence. He has tried to balance the budget at inopportune moments—the 1937-38 adventure in "economy" resulted in a sudden economic down-spiral that was barely checked in time. (I am not against "economy," but you can't take digitalis away from a cardiac with impunity.) Finally, the President's court packing plan of 1937 was indefensible: even senators who went along with Roosevelt here for various ulterior motives of their own admit that the plan was "dumb."

The court pack plan was indefensible not because Roosevelt didn't have a perfect right to ask for court enlargement but because of the specious grounds upon which he chose to fight. Had the pack gone through, a precedent would have been created for the Republicans.

Luckily for the nation, Senator Burton Wheeler's courageous stand against the plan has resulted in insuring us a liberal court for a decade to come. For after their appeals to morality and the Constitution during the long Winter of 1937, the Republicans would certainly not dare to pack the court of Frankfurter, Reed, Black, Douglas, Murphy and Stone should the New Deal lose at the polls next Autumn. About the only good thing that can be said for the court pack attempt is that it put a scissors on Mr. Justice Roberts, who switched to the liberal side in 1937 just in time to save some essential New Deal legislation.

None of Roosevelt's inner circle really approved the court plan: Bob Jackson, Tommy Corcoran and the rest "went along" merely because of their conception of loyalty to the "skipper." And Roosevelt himself has inferentially condemned the circumlocutory and hypocritical *method* which Homer Cummings, his then attorney general, cooked up for him at the tag end of 1936. In Emil Ludwig's biography of Roosevelt there is an anecdote that reveals the President's more sober attitude toward his own besetting weakness. . . . Once the youthful Franklin, hurrying to catch a train in Boston, barged full-tilt into an Italian boy and knocked him down. The friends of the Italian boy came rushing up, and Roosevelt, to get away, pulled a propitiatory dollar from his pocket. The crowd immediately yelled "bribery." They snarled and threatened to punch the young aristocrat in the face. Finally, Franklin seized his valise, made a quick breakaway, and clambered out of the reach of menacing fists just as the train was pulling out. "The whole trouble," said Roosevelt later, "was that I didn't solve the problem. I tried to dodge it by creating a diversion. That doesn't work. I'll never try it again." But he did try it again, with the "diversion" of the court pack bill. And, once more, the trick failed him. Whereas a straightforward attack on the court, as counseled by Tom Corcoran, Ben Cohen and Robert Jackson, would almost certainly have commanded the moral prestige to get the crucial borderline votes.

Roosevelt's relish for a too clever trick is his least pleasant characteristic. But the defect is probably inseparable from the Rooseveltian qualities. The President loves politics as a game. When you are playing a game you make use of the ruse and the feint: the whole concept of political timing is an unmoral concept, for the moral man always tells you where he stands regardless of the possible consequences. Roosevelt's passion for politics inevitably involves a suspension of moral criteria at certain times. Yet if he lacked the passion for politics as an art, he would be as defenseless as a lobster without a shell. From the Rooseveltian love of the game as a game comes the power of refreshment and renewal. If Roosevelt couldn't delight in a trick or two, he would not last very long to carry the fight forward. So, taking the best with the worst, all we can say is that Franklin

Delano Roosevelt's virtues as a party leader on the domestic front have outweighed his faults.

Moreover, there has been a broad and sometimes unwitting consistency in the Rooseveltian career so far as domestic policies go. When Walter Lippmann portrayed the President as a weak waverer back in 1932, he spoke without knowledge of the man's political past. Roosevelt's tactics as governor of New York during the Walker-Seabury fight looked like the soul of timidity at the time. But as Jimmy the Well-Dressed Mayor twisted and turned and betrayed himself by his deviousness, the Roosevelt inertia in the face of the Seabury charges of municipal corruption in New York City began to look like inexorable glacial pressure. Roosevelt simply let Walker and Tammany kill themselves. If he had actively interfered in the fight, he would have made it impossible for Jim Farley to operate on his behalf later on in campaigning for Manhattan district votes for a Rooseveltian national ticket. In politics you don't make unnecessary enemies.

Roosevelt has always had his "Dutch." When he was a state senator in Albany in the days before the World War, he led an insurgent Democratic revolt against the organization choice of Blue-Eyed Billy Sheehan for United States senator. Mauritz Hallgren objects that Roosevelt, in fighting Sheehan, didn't know that he was in reality fighting a bankers' clique. But Roosevelt did know that he was fighting against the choice of a man whose interests were exclusively metropolitan. Roosevelt, the squire from the land, wanted a better balance between city and country interests in his senator. The germ of the New Deal, which was designed primarily to even things up between the plutocratic city and the impoverished country, between metropolitan East and plundered West and South, can be discovered in this early fight.

If you will read the first volume of the collected public papers and addresses of the President which his friend, Judge Samuel I. ("Sammy the Rose") Rosenman, has edited, you will discover that Roosevelt certainly knew the identity of his enemies when he was governor of New York State. Was Al Smith's successor at Albany an "amiable" philanthropist in his attitude toward the use of state water power by unrestricted privately owned public utilities? His speeches and messages on the subject do not exactly pulse with an "eagerness" to please Hopson or Insull or any of the old utility kings. His record on labor legislation as governor is progressive enough; so is his record on housing, on the relief of unemployment and on rural land utilization. The New Deal was implicit in practically all his speeches and activities as governor; even the unfortunate word "stabilization"—the *ignis fatuus* that led to NRA—crops up in a couple of reports on industry. Only one speech of his pre-presidential years can live to plague Roosevelt, and that is the campaign address on the Federal budget, delivered at Pittsburgh on October 9, 1932. In this speech Roosevelt, of all people, accused Herbert Hoover of having unbalanced the budget. But, in justice to Roosevelt, the accusation boils down to this: the Republicans had been lax about using the taxing power to reduce the national debt when they had the chance, and they had even refunded money to corporations that were rolling in wealth at the time. Roosevelt's own idea even then was more or less John Maynard Keynes's: balance the budget and reduce the debt when you can, but forget (temporarily) the orthodox banker's idea of governmental finance when relief requirements, the stop-gap alleviation of human misery, demand it.

John T. Flynn complains that Roosevelt has never made the most of his opportunities on the domestic front. But history will record that the President always went from the worse to the better until the European war distracted him. It is perfectly true that the SEC under Joe Kennedy and Jim Landis was innocuous. But after Kennedy and Landis came Fighting Bill Douglas (who would make an admirable President), and after Douglas came Jerome Frank, who is both tactful and unafraid. The NRA was a blue-print for a slave economy. But NRA flopped; and with its failure the disciples of Brandeis and Felix Frankfurter—the Corcorans, Cohens, Bob Jacksons and Leon Hendersons—took control. These men, as I shall endeavor to demonstrate in another chapter, believe in a free capitalist, decentralist economy. Many business men refuse to see this. But by the same token many business men secretly believe in monopoly, in NRA-ism, in Big Business Fascism. Corcoran, Cohen, Jackson and Henderson are old-fashioned Populist radicals who are making the attempt to redefine Populism—or a free business system created in the image of the small man —in terms of modern technological realities. Roosevelt has his occasional lapses into an NRA psychology. But when he advocates small steel mills for New England —mills that will utilize Cuban and South American ore shipped by water—he is talking the Brandeis language. When he hopes to see many new small farmers making use of Grand Coulee electric power to make the State of Washington desert reaches blossom as the rose, he is also talking the Brandeis language. History will record that he took good advice when he allowed the Brandeiseans to run his economic show.

The trouble is, he began late; and never permitted himself a final clarification of long-term objectives. As we have seen in our analysis of the structure of the Democratic Party, the political horse-traders in the Rooseveltian Congresses were inclined to call it a deal when AAA was swapped for Relief—stop-gap measures that feed people in trouble yet fail to give sharecroppers or unemployed workers a new *productive* stake in the economic system. In 1933 Roosevelt appropriately recognized the right of everyone to consume in a rich nation where there is certainly enough to go around. But how the dispossessed are to be rehabilitated as producers he has never clearly indicated. Rex Tugwell once had the glimmering of an idea in Rural Resettlement, but Mr. Tugwell was too much of a total planner to get along with the more pluralistic Henry Wallace. Action on the railroads has been postponed all through the two Roosevelt administrations; and investment in housing has never moved appreciably. Fear of *rentier* pressure groups, of insurance company investors, of real estate racketeers and of the building trades unions, paralyzed the New Deal where drastic action would obviously have resulted in new investment and new employment—maybe, even, a real boom. Fear of "losing" cotton and wheat overseas markets that were already gone beyond redemption kept the Department of Agriculture from a crusade to bring dairying into the South, and a return to cattle and sheep raising on the high plains. The monopoly question in the heavy industries agitated some of the New Dealers for years before any real study of administered prices and patent-law bottlenecks was even authorized. And it was not until 1939 that a Supreme Court decision made it illegal for finagling stockholders to cut into the "prior lien" of the bondholders during bankruptcy reorganizations.

History will record that the New Deal trembled on the verge of a real new deal—and drew back. Franklin Delano Roosevelt is far more sophisticated than his famous fifth-cousin Theodore ever was. But, as Henry R. Luce has remarked, Roosevelt II lacks Roosevelt I's power of imaginative projection. T.R.'s career as a

cow-puncher, a buccaneering power-politics land-grab-
ber in the Philippines and the Canal Zone, a conserva-
tionist, a U. S. A. booster and a trust-fighter may make
much or little sense historically. But at least it gives
you a fair picture of what Americans were dreaming
about in the 1900-14 period. FDR's activities and
speeches give only a partial picture of our dreams: to
get at the core of the New Deal you have to look at
people as diverse as Mordecai Ezekiel, Leon Henderson, Bill Douglas, Tom Corcoran and Felix Frankfurter, all of whom have pushed adventurously into
realms that the "skipper" himself has never been
willing to explore. Roosevelt's willingness to keep both
Donald Richberg and Leon Henderson on tap as economic advisers even during his second term is eloquent
of a final fuzziness of aim.

The final confusion of the New Deal is apparent in
the alacrity with which Roosevelt has welcomed the
European war as an excuse for an attempted reorienta-
tion of his party. The cry for "unity" is a specious cry;
we are not at war with anybody, and our home problems demand argument, not "unity." I don't mean to
imply by this criticism that Roosevelt likes war; and I
am willing to grant that his famous Chautauqua speech
denouncing war was quite sincere. But it is far easier to
lecture Hitler than to fight for a repeal of the poll tax
in Mississippi, far easier to advocate a new Wilsonian-
ism in international affairs than to purge Senator Pat
Harrison. When you spend $80,000,000 on a Bonne-

ville Dam to harness the water power of the Columbia River, you have to justify the expense to business men in Portland and to stump-ranchers in the Oregon back-country, both of which groups will complain of waste if they don't get quick results from the new dynamos. And you have to justify the expense to taxpayers who are yelling for economy and a balanced budget. But when you spend $80,000,000 on a new battleship there is little outcry. The battleship may be necessary or it may not be necessary, but in any event it is a floating sacred cow of the sea.

As I shall endeavor to show, I have no objection to the Hull reciprocal trade pacts. But I do object to the type of mind that sees Mr. Hull as the key figure in the administration instead of someone operating on the periphery. Foreign trade may be worth having, but foreign trade has little "leverage" value for the U. S. economy as a whole if it is unaccompanied by foreign lending.

All of which brings us to State Department policy. Mr. Roosevelt has pretty much given Mr. Hull his head ever since the departure from Washington of Raymond Moley. Now, Mr. Hull is a saint. But this particular saint is surrounded by smooth operators who like to think of such institutions as the international tin and rubber cartels, both of which "administer" their prices, as "free" competitors in a "free" world trading community. When Mr. Hull arranges a loan to Brazil to stymie the Nazi successors of Dr. Schacht, he is against "tying" clauses. He is against *specific* loans, say, for the development of rubber culture in the Amazon valley, or for the building of a tin smelter in the western hemisphere to make use of Bolivian ores. He is against a specific loan for the exploitation of Brazilian manganese. Any such "interference" would disrupt the "normal" channels of trade that send us to the East Indies for tin and rubber and to Russia for manganese.

Such high-mindedness would make perfect sense *if* we had a Manchester free trade world even west of the Rhine. But in the context of world-trade-as-it-is, the high-mindedness of Mr. Hull actually helps to throttle competition. Mr. Hull might at least use the *threat* of tying-clause loans to wangle better prices from international cartels for American business men. A rubber supply in the Amazon basin would, of course, be an advantage to us in case the Malay States get involved in a Pacific war between Britain and the Japanese. But it would also foster competition between two parts of the colonial world for American markets in Akron— and the American automobile owner would be the gainer. If Mr. Hull were interested in the philosophy of the New Deal instead of in an abstraction taken long ago from the economic textbooks of his youth he might see this. But Mr. Hull has never shown any interest whatsoever in the newer domestic problems of the United States. As Eliot Janeway has pointed out, the State Department and the New Deal have never been formally introduced to each other.

The tragedy of all this is not Mr. Hull's tragedy; it is Roosevelt's. For the President has allowed himself to be shanghaied—by Mr. Hull.

Sooner or later Roosevelt will see this; he always does come around in time. In early 1939 he was straining to range us on one side in the European conflict; in the Autumn he caught the ground-tone of the American people and pulled back to a fairly sound neutrality-plus-cash-and-carry position. But the second-term sands are running out, and soon it will be too late for this administration to do anything creative even in the propagandistic sense.

We come inevitably to the question of the third term. I have no doubt that Roosevelt can have the Democratic nomination if he wants it. Moreover, he can probably win at the polls in November against a couple of Republicans named Joe. But, assuming that Roosevelt is sincere in his desire to see the U. S. keep out of the European war, I don't know why he should want a third term for himself. He would begin his new Presidency with a fairly unsympathetic Congress: only a third of the Senate is up for re-election this year, which means the New Deal can't gain appreciably in the upper house; and the temper of the country would hardly express itself in a wildly pro-New Deal House of Representatives. If a President can do little in a second term, he can do nothing at all in a third term—that is, unless he is to be a candidate for a *fourth* term and hence a power to be propitiated. (When we begin talking about fourth terms, however, it begins to smack of totalitarianism.) The next four years will probably see a consolidation of most of the New Deal gains no matter who is elected; but so far as experimentation goes they will be plateau years. And they will probably see the next major economic recession. Roosevelt's great value is that he has started something that will go on with increased momentum only when the people have had enough of marking time and looking anxiously at Europe. Why, then, should he put himself in a position to take the blame for a period of mild reaction and an economic depression? If the Democratic Party is going to function as a conservative party, why head it? Why not join the fructifying opposition? There is a time for everything; and 1941-44 is no time for a Roosevelt to be President unless he merely wants to be President. He should keep his reputation clean for 1944—when a Bull Moose ticket, or a La Follette ticket, or a Bill Douglas ticket, may be in order.

As a matter of fact, no liberals seem to be available for 1940—and if Roosevelt is himself available (as he is) it is as a conservative Roosevelt, not as a New Dealer. Can the La Follettes do anything this year? Patently, no. Can Bill Douglas? He lacks a machine. Can Frank Murphy? He is a Catholic. Can Harry Hopkins, or Robert H. Jackson, or Henry Wallace? They lack strength back in the counties that send the delegates to the state nominating conventions; and besides, if any of them threatened to win the Democratic nomination the Garner forces would probably "take a walk." There is only one liberal in the country at the moment with any power of maneuver, and, paradoxically, he is nominally a Republican. His name is Fiorello H. La Guardia.

Let us look, therefore, at La Guardia in his native setting, the cosmopolis of New York. This city, according to Rexford Guy Tugwell, head of Mayor La Guardia's City Planning Commission, is shrinking up as a port; there are thousands in the city who will never find work there again. Once the queen metropolis of this hemisphere, gateway for throngs of immigrants, and shipping center for two-thirds of the nation's hinterland, it is fast becoming a city on the periphery of a continent. Economic nationalism is the villain; despite Cordell Hull's most gallant efforts, our foreign commerce has never risen in recent years to the high points of the Twenties, and what there is of it is likely to clear through Houston-Galveston or Baltimore— though the Port of New York may still hold the bulk of the passenger and mail service. With the carrying trade dispersed or lethargic, there are more than 600,000 unemployed in New York City—about a sixteenth of the total for the entire United States.

If you go with Mr. Tugwell to the top of New York City's Municipal Building, you may be treated to a packed five-minute lesson in the sociology of urban change that is worth a full course at the University of Chicago, where they study the subject more intensively than elsewhere. From Mr. Tugwell's eyrie, New York is an inspiring sight: the tall buildings rise into the enchanted air from a misty plain of red brick and brownstone; even the most garish things are softened by distance. Beyond the island of Manhattan, the rivers and the bay are the same thrilling setting that made Ernest Poole's "The Harbor" one of the memorable books of pre-war America. But Mr. Tugwell, who is an ironist, bids you forget the aerial perspectives and memories of "The Harbor." His finger stabs at Al Smith's East Side—a huddle of tenements which is startlingly interrupted by the adventure in practical idealism that is Knickerbocker Village. Then he points to distant Queens, which is lost in the haze beyond the graceful arcs of the Williamsburg Bridge. In Queens and the Bronx, Knickerbocker Village would be just another new development: people are deserting Manhattan to live in the newer boroughs. New York is like other American metropolises, like Chicago with its tenement-encircled loop: as it burgeons on the periphery it decays, like an overripe apple, just around the core.

"Well and good," you may say; "decentralization is a fine thing, and the children will have more light and air." But that is not Mr. Tugwell's point for the moment. For as the city ripples outward towards the horizons, the cost *per capita* of servicing the population rises steeply. Subways must continue to stop at Canal and Bleecker streets; white wings must sweep the gutters: the servicing of the inner city must go on at approximately the same total cost regardless of population decrease in that area. Yet every new apartment, every new adventure in "planned overcrowding," every new decentralized factory, in Queens and the Bronx adds to the service bill for New York City as a whole. Meanwhile the assessments on inner city real estate must be maintained. For New York City is limited by state law to a debt of ten per cent of its real estate assessment, and to an annual tax not to exceed two per cent of this assessment. The annual budget for New York runs close to $600,000,000—and the city is already within $37,000,000 of its legal debt limit. Cut down on the traditional assessments of East Side property and you strike a mortal blow at New York's ability to raise even the minimum of tax money that is required to take care of a population of 7,500,000, including the 600,000 unemployed.

As the municipality is frantically striving to protect its tax base, the landlords of the inner city grasp at straws. They can't afford improvements, for the assessments might be increased. If new buildings are to be built, they must go up on cheaper land in Queens, in Brooklyn, in the Bronx. A queer paradox: the City Planning Commission cannot plan effectively for the inner city, for if it did it would have to cut into the very real estate assessments that enable Mayor La Guardia to pay Mr. Tugwell's salary. Yet there is an even stranger paradox. Descending from the Municipal Building, let us go to Washington, D. C., where New York's whilom city chamberlain, Adolf Berle, now holds forth in the State Department. Berle's keen face —the face of a sensitive and weary fox—lights up at mention of New York City. New York, he says, has become a real cosmopolis since 1933—the cultural capital of what remains of Western civilization. The glories of contemporary New York are not in the least dependent on Mr. Whalen's Fair; the city is changing as old "El" structures are ripped down, as Robert Moses plants thousands of trees in its parks, as the Henry Hudson Parkway and the Triborough Bridge and the West Side Highway help clear the streets of exacerbated motorists. The city is changing, too, as the refugees of the arts from Central Europe give it an almost Parisian intellectual flavor. If Berle is in an expansive mood, he may remind you of the finale of the opera "Louise," with the crashing chords of "Par-ee, Par-ee," an expression of heart-breaking love for city life and city vistas.

The cultural capital of Western civilization? A decaying port on the periphery of a continent? On the face of it, the two things would seem to be incompatible. Yet the odd thing about it is that Tugwell's city is also Berle's city; and the great reconciler who has succeeded in the face of shrunken resources in creating the one out of the other is New York's ebullient Latin

Mayor, Fiorello H. La Guardia of Italy, Arizona, Budapest, and way stations.

Fiorello Henry (for Enrico) La Guardia was born for politics. The most obvious thing to say about him is that he combines many of the elements that once made Theodore Roosevelt an irresistible public figure: a mixed metropolitan and Far Western background, a military interlude in his past, a contempt for red tape, a love for the effective gesture and grimace, a talent for dramatic strenuosity. But Fiorello, the Little Flower of Manhattan, has other things which T.R. never had. With all of his ranching and grizzly-hunting and Rough Riding, the first Roosevelt never really understood the dirt farmer west of the Populist crusade, or the homespun democratic aspirations of an Altgeld, a Bryan, a La Follette. La Guardia, on the other hand, knows that fifty-cent wheat does not jibe with six per cent mortgages and high land valuation; he proved it during his terms as Congressman in the Twenties, when he constituted himself a spokesman for the wheatlands even though his supporters lived largely in East Harlem. Again, Theodore Roosevelt made himself the conscious spokesman of melting-pot America. But La Guardia *is* melting-pot America—first generation Italian-American, with a Jewish great-great-grandparent lending a posthumous dynamism to the winged La Guardian denunciations of Hitler.

When a politician trims his sails to the wind and compromises the full demands of his strongest supporters in order to save at least some parts of a program, he is frequently greeted with cries of "sell-out." Yet, to function at all, democracy depends on the politician performing just such a broker service for his people. The good politician must be both a representative of the part and a flexible member of the Committee of the Whole—a paradoxical position that can be held only by artists who trust their observations and intuitions more than they trust formal logic. Once in a lifetime we get a superior broker-politician, such as Franklin Roosevelt, for President—a man who knows when it is practical to think in the particularist terms of labor, or the unemployed, or the Navy League, and when it is necessary to compromise the particular for the sake of the general. Coming down from Mr. Roosevelt, we find only a few similar master brokers of politics. There is Frank Murphy of Michigan, who managed in 1937 both to represent labor and to play the role of honest mediator between Walter Chrysler and John L. Lewis. There are the two La Follettes. But the most skillful master broker below the office of President is Fiorello La Guardia, who, as Mayor, is both a very effective particularist for his immediate followers (New York's large Italian and Jewish populations and New York labor in so far as it thinks of itself as a class), and a rip-roaring Committee of the Whole for New York City all by himself.

Moreover, La Guardia, though only a Mayor at the moment, is conspicuously able to think in national

terms. He knows that economics is a matter of reciprocal relationships and interstitial adjustments; he would
never make the mistake of a Calvin Coolidge and support a high protective tariff while vetoing a McNary-
Haugen Bill for the protection of agriculture. Unlike
an older generation of eastern liberal, the generation
of Theodore Roosevelt, Mayor La Guardia states his
moral convictions in economic terms. But the moralism
is there, a conspicuous part of the La Guardian make-up.
La Guardia is no purist when it comes to electioneer-
ing; he has always kept his fences in good repair, he
knows a thing or two about pre-convention trickery, and
he has never been contemptuous of the value of a well-
oiled political machine. But he is fanatically moral
about two things: he will take no campaign contribu-
tions from sources that might prove prejudicial to a
free hand later on, and he invariably opposes the
spread of an easy-money philosophy among his under-
lings and constituents. One of the first things La
Guardia did as Mayor of New York was to fire a
deputy commissioner for the trivial sin of presenting a
load of City gravel to a Boy Scout camp. And as a
member of Congress in 1932, La Guardia opposed the
Soldiers' Bonus. Unlike some Rooseveltians, the Mayor
has stated his conviction that large-scale relief payments
are only a short-term palliative; they must be made
unnecessary if democracy is not to be strangled by debt.
In stating his conviction on this score, the Mayor can
hardly be accused of pandering to the unemployed

pressure groups that are becoming more and more of an election-day factor. Yet he is politically wise in dissociating himself from the "gimme" psychology, for when "production" inevitably replaces "distribution" as the watchword of progressive politics La Guardia will be in a position to capitalize on the change.

Since La Guardia undeniably loves to sun himself in the full gaze of the multitude, it is easy to make out a case against his "demagoguery." Like Coolidge before him, he has allowed himself to be dressed in the feathered panoply of Indian tribesmen. The Mayor is an adept in all branches of political fanfaronade: he can lead the Fire Department Band, he can dress up in a sand-hog's helmet to inspect new tunnels, he can step into the pitcher's box on opening day at the Yankee Stadium and cut loose with a high, hard one in the general direction of home plate. A virtuoso in exploiting his temperament, he can be charming one moment and thunderclap-angry the next. But if you watch the Mayor closely, you will discover that his dramatics are generally functional: they have the intent of a parable. Back in 1925, when living costs were mounting in New York City, La Guardia took the floor in the House of Representatives and started pulling lamb chops from his pockets. His colleagues tittered and sat up. But this was only the beginning of an illustrated lecture, for the next thing La Guardia produced from his person was a steak. After elaborating on the high price of sirloin, La Guardia then materialized an entire three-dollar roast. "What workman's family can afford to pay three dollars for a roast of this size?" asked La Guardia, waving it in the faces of the amazed representatives. "What are we coming to? . . . It is high time that this matter of price-fixing be stopped. . . ." The Chicago packers saw very little to laugh at in such clowning. But they couldn't dismiss it as meaningless demagoguery, for the New York meat strike which followed in the wake of La Guardia's exhibitionism pulled the price of lamb chops and roasts down considerably.

Since La Guardia has become Mayor of New York, this sort of pertinent dramatic "business" has been an almost daily occurrence. For example, when one of La Guardia's commissioners does something stupid, the Mayor presents him with a piece of well-polished bone. Fire Commissioner McElligott once earned the bone when, after delivering a lecture on a safe-and-sane Fourth of July, he went home to burn his hand lighting firecrackers. If the Mayor happens to discover that his police captains have been oversleeping in the morning, he presents them with dollar alarm clocks. The horseplay that goes on in City Hall frequently reminds one of life in a prep school dormitory. But the La Guardian tricks usually have the aim of promoting efficient service; Horatio Alger would have understood them.

The astoundingly clever little Italian-American politico who can turn his charm or his anger or his ingenuity on and off at will was born in New York City on December 11, 1882. His father, Achille, was the son of Rafael Enrico La Guardia, who had become a Protestant to fight the Papal Troops as one of Garibaldi's freedom-loving Red Shirts. A composer, conductor, and cornetist, Achille La Guardia originally visited the United States as an accompanist for Adelina Patti. He remained here to take up a career as army bandmaster—which, in the days of the "old" army, meant a life spent at frontier posts on the great plains and in the Far West.

With his father, Fiorello La Guardia left his native city of New York when he was three years old and did not see it again until he was a young man. Meanwhile, he drank in the tradition of the old pioneer West, first at Fort Sully in South Dakota and later at Whipple Barracks near Prescott in what was then the Arizona Territory. "Prescott," La Guardia says, "was really my home town; we lived there until the Spanish-American War started the troops moving again." It was at Prescott that Fiorello finished grammar school and went to high school; and it was in his mother's Arizona kitchen that he learned the art of making tempting sauces for spaghetti, a forte that now serves him as his once-a-week prime hobby. His musical father brought Fiorello up to play the cornet and taught him to love Italian opera, but the patriotic bandmaster refused to give his children the opportunity to learn the Italian language. Hence it was not until he went to Fiume as U. S. consular agent at the age of twenty that Fiorello learned to speak his father's native tongue.

The mystery of what makes one man a conservative and another a liberal will probably never be solved. Certain it is that the old West was a democratic society, the matrix of the frontier progressivism of men like George Norris and the elder La Follette. But the old West also produced conservatives of the stripe of the late Senator Warren of Wyoming, whose acquisitive love for his flocks earned him the title of Greatest Shepherd since Abraham. As an army post boy, Fiorello might have grown up to worship regimentation, authority, "orders from above"; he might have been predisposed to Mussolini. The fact remains, however, that La Guardia took from the American West what the Norrises and the La Follettes have taken from it; he became a humanitarian and a democrat.

But if one were asked to name the most important influence in the life of Fiorello La Guardia as a public servant, one would be tempted to say "embalmed beef." For it was putrefied rations sold in 1898 by conscienceless contractors to the army at Tampa that killed Achille La Guardia and turned young Fiorello out into the world to support himself and his mother. To this day attempts to "gyp" the government and the taxpayers fill Fiorello La Guardia with a cold rage; the success of his invective against Tammany Hall can probably be traced back to the embalmed beef episode.

For a short time during the Spanish-American War,

The American Stakes

Fiorello was an unsalaried correspondent of the *St. Louis Dispatch*. His first real job, however, was civil service, with the American consulate at Budapest. Soon he was consular agent in Fiume, then a nominally Hungarian city; and soon he was deep in the study of Italian, German, and Croatian. As a consul, La Guardia insisted on medical inspection of prospective emigrants to the United States at the point of embarkation. This meant that physically defective people were turned down at Fiume instead of at Ellis Island, and the steamship companies were thus deprived of some passage money. When the Cunard Line objected, La Guardia held his ground. Twenty years later, as a member of Congress, La Guardia was to vote for a measure that officially inaugurated the system which he himself had started at Fiume as a young man of twenty-one.

The excitement of living in Europe had worn off by the time La Guardia was twenty-four; so he resigned in 1906 from the consular service and returned at long last to his native city of New York. But, as Paul Kern says, it was not a home-coming. La Guardia was still a Westerner, and the sight of the slums, the treeless streets, the pullulating waterfront, and the political tactics of Tammany Hall created a bitter resentment in this stranger who had known the freedom of Arizona and the graciousness of Budapest. Eager to get on, La Guardia first took up shorthand. This, coupled with his linguistic facility, got him a job as Ellis Island interpreter—and opportunity to add Yiddish, French, and Spanish to his repertory. His evenings were spent studying law at New York University, where he took his LL.B. in 1910. Admitted to the bar that same year, he Anglicized his middle name to Henry and hung out a shingle. When the cases failed to come in, he went out and looked for them—and found his first real clients among the garment workers during the great strikes of 1912 and 1913.

Try as he might, La Guardia could not keep from gravitating into the public service. If he had lived in a Republican community, he would undoubtedly have become a Bryan Democrat. But since he lived in Greenwich Village, in a district set aside by Tammany as home base for New York City's Congressional representative of the liquor lobby, La Guardia naturally became a Progressive Republican. Bipartisan deals were common in his district, with the Republicans usually winking as they nominated a nonentity for Congress. They winked once too often when they made up the slate for 1914, with La Guardia named to oppose Tammany's Michael Farley. Quite innocent of any "deal," La Guardia scurried about the lower East Side stretches of his district, speaking Croatian to Slavs, German to Germans, Yiddish to Jews, and Italian to Neapolitans. Farley, of course, won the election. But the Republicans opened their eyes on the morning after election day, for their "nonentity" had corralled 14,000 votes which normally had gone into the Tammany column. As a reward for his vote-getting La Guardia was appointed Deputy State Attorney General by Republican Albany. Two years later he beat Tammany to the draw by mobilizing his friends among the garment workers and the letter-carriers and by pulling the flop-house vote out of bed long before the Tammany workers had risen for the day. Stunned by this bare-faced theft of their own tactics, Tammany failed to recover in time to count La Guardia out; and the swarthy, stocky young man from the West with the high-pitched voice and the smoldering energy of two people found himself victor over Farley by 257 votes. The year was 1916, and America was starting down the road to war. Forehanded as always, La Guardia took lessons in flying out at Mineola before going off to Washington. When war was declared, he resigned his seat to become the "flying Congressman," captain of American aviators in Italy.

Things went swiftly for La Guardia during the next few years. As a captain of aviation he showed particular genius in cutting army red tape, contriving to get food, gasoline, safe planes, and venereal prophylaxis for his men in spite of written regulations, Roman bureaucrats, and—in the case of the prophylaxis—the timid objections of his medical officer. After the disaster of Caporetto, La Guardia was detailed to rally Italians— in Italian. He returned with decorations and the rank of major, and in 1918 he went back to Congress. When Al Smith quit the presidency of New York City's Board of Aldermen to become Governor of the State, the Republicans naturally picked their only Manhattan vote-getter to run for the vacant chair. The "Major" won, as usual, and marched down to New York's lovely colonial city hall to contract a strange alliance with Democratic Mayor "Red Mike" Hylan against Tammany men who called him Blackguardia. But just as life seemed most serene, the luck turned completely. First, the Republicans, who had promised to nominate him for Mayor in 1921, decided he was too radical for the job. Then, after defeat in the primaries, La Guardia was compelled to undergo an operation for an old war wound at the base of his spine. Then burglars rifled his new home on University Avenue in the Bronx, and then his new baby daughter, Fioretta, died. A month later his wife—Thea Almerigotti, who had kept her promise and married him when the Italians recovered Trieste—succumbed to tuberculosis. La Guardia, in the Autumn of 1921, was a thoroughly beaten man.

Those who counted him out, however, were reckoning without his resilience and his habit of seeking anodyne in work. In 1922 the La Guardia Stetson was back in the ring; the "damn little demagogue" literally blackmailed the Republicans into nominating him for Congressman for a Harlem district by threatening to run as an independent candidate against Nathan L. Miller for Governor. Tammany countered by picking a prominent Jew to run for Congress in East Harlem, and then spread the libel that the Major was anti-Semitic. That particular canard made La Guardia furious, but it was easily disposed of by an invitation to his opponent to debate in Yiddish. Since La Guardia knew his rival knew no Yiddish, the offer was perfectly safe —but just to carry things off with flair La Guardia did deliver his side of the debate in Yiddish anyway. His district being predominantly Jewish and Italian—the two strains of his ancestry—he held it for five terms running. Not until 1932, after Tammany-manipulated Puerto Ricans had edged a number of habitual La Guardia supporters out of East Harlem, did the Major taste defeat.

La Guardia's years as a Congressman were spent in apparently fruitless opposition. For a whole decade he scratched, kicked, and bit at the Drys. He attacked Andrew Mellon's ideas on taxation, carried on a one-man fight against the corruption of the federal judiciary, opposed Congressional pork in all its forms, and helped keep Muscle Shoals out of the hands of Henry Ford without managing to substitute government operation for private exploitation. Though a war veteran himself, La Guardia refused to become a leader in the American Legion, and he opposed any increase in the size of the army. On child labor legislation and the woman's suffrage amendment he managed to be on the winning side.

But La Guardia didn't care about quick and easy victories; he knew the Twenties were coming to an end. Almost alone in the House he took the market crash of 1929 for what it was, the real end of an era. He sailed into Insull and Richard Whitney—"unfairly," as it seemed to many at the time. Later on, his remarks about the "banketeers" seemed prophetic.

Prophetic, too, were the campaign speeches he delivered while running in 1929 against James J. Walker for Mayor. La Guardia had no chance against the debonaire Jimmy that year, but he used his opportunity to make some long-term political "character" for himself by anticipating the incredible findings of the Seabury investigations. Soon after La Guardia's 1929 defeat, the "tin box brigade" was admitting colossal graft charges, and soon Walker was off for Europe. The New York newspapers that had called La Guardia "irresponsible" in 1929 were compelled to print story after story about political graft in markets, traction and bus franchises, sewer construction, condemnation proceedings, what-not.

Tammany might still have held New York City had it not been for La Guardia's prescience in 1932 and 1933; with an army of office-holders to hold entire families and the old Christmas-box tradition to hold the ever numerous poor, the Tiger might have waited while Seabury howled. But when Tammany was electing Judge O'Brien to finish out Jimmy Walker's term, La Guardia took careful note of the apparently spontaneous McKee "write-in" vote. That vote, he was certain, represented a new Mugwump stratification; it could be had by a courageous "fusion" candidate. Unfortunately, the Republicans weren't asking for courage; they wanted to nominate someone "safe" in 1933. La Guardia, however, had impressed Judge Seabury; and people like Adolf Berle were willing to testify that the Major had a real mind and a real talent for constructive work as well as an oppositionist's voice. With some difficulty Judge Seabury put La Guardia across with the reformers' Committee of Fourteen—and La Guardia went on to win. On January 1, 1934, he became the ninety-ninth Mayor of the city of his birth. Two years later he was re-elected, the first reform candidate to invalidate the old chestnut about Tammany being the sea and reform only a wave. But this time he needed the help of a new political party—the American Labor Party—to put him over.

As an executive, La Guardia has had his troubles, some of which were self-imposed. To begin with, he was entirely ineffective at first in the job of delegating detail to others. If he had kept on as he started in 1934, he would have killed himself with meaningless overwork long before this—though, often enough, he still works a sixteen-hour day. Secondly, his temper frequently got the better of him: he expected miracles from his commissioners, his secretaries, and from the city hall reporters. Gradually, however, he has learned the requirements of executive work; and he has also learned to curb his tongue. Since his marriage to Marie Fischer, who used to be his secretary in Washington, he has adopted two children. He gets needed relaxation from playing with them on the sands at Westport—and from going to concerts and baseball games when he can.

Moreover, though he could not quite believe it at first, his commissioners are an exceptionally able lot; La Guardia really can delegate authority. Some of the La Guardia "cabinet" men were picked from outside New York City, notably Health Commissioner John Rice, who had made the Department of Health in New Haven the most effective in the United States. Robert Moses, the Park Commissioner—conservative in his politics and entirely autocratic in his methods—has been a wonder at accomplishment. The label in politics means nothing to La Guardia: his Investigation Commissioner, Paul Blanshard, was formerly a Norman Thomas Socialist. For Fire and Police heads, La Guardia eventually chose deserving—as contrasted with "deserving"—men from the departmental ranks. But the Mayor, who knows that a politician is useless for good unless he can continue to hold office, did not push "purity" to quixotic extremes: when he could give a job to a "deserving" man who happened to be honest and fairly efficient as well he did not let his scruples become fantastic.

In any event, the effect of La Guardia on New York City has been tremendous. Money has been saved by the rigorous economies of the newly created central purchasing agency, and by the simpler device of separating club-house loafers from the city pay roll. Scientific valuation of utilities has spread the tax base of a city already suffering from the decline of its real estate.

And money has been gained by a sales tax—of which La Guardia has said, "It is wholly wrong except for one thing—it raises the money we need." New York Civil Service, now under the capable administration of Paul Kern, is—as Mr. Kern quite immodestly puts it— "99 and 44/100 per cent pure," with almost twice as many highly paid jobs covered by competitive rules as used to be the case under Tammany. As for the new parks, the new highways, the new hospital facilities, the new low-cost housing developments, the new sewage-disposal plants, the new school seats, the improvement of transit, the new airport at North Beach, New York City owes a great deal to largesse from Washington. But not everything: for though the New Deal has poured a neat billion into New York since 1934, the city treasury itself has had to drum up $800,000,000 to get the billion. And this in the face of Tugwell's paradox.

Where can a man like La Guardia go when he decides to quit being Mayor of his home town? If we are going to become conscious of "race," he can go nowhere. But on the assumption that "race" can hardly be a real issue in a nation with democratic melting-pot traditions, La Guardia has the same chance as other good non-party men in politics. He is certainly not an "available" candidate for the Presidency, the Vice-Presidency, the New York governorship, or the U. S. Senate. Although it bears the Republican tag, his progressivism is closer to Roosevelt's Democracy than it is to anything that may be found in the eastern Republican ranks. A hundred years ago, when John C. Calhoun left the Jacksonian party to become a temporary Whig, cross-overs were possible in American politics. Today they are extremely difficult. With the Republicans against him and the Roosevelt Democrats unable to accept him, La Guardia is on a ticklish spot. Like the machineless Frank Murphy, like the Third Party La Follettes, like the "Independent" George Norris, he must depend entirely on personality and wits—and on his ability to ride the lightning when it is about to strike.

Nevertheless, such a position is not hopeless: one quite orthodox way of getting things done in American politics is to break all the rules of "regularity." La Guardia has always been orthodoxly unorthodox—and he has held office for two decades with only a few months' break. Given a Democratic débâcle in the Autumn of 1940 and a victory for the more sterile sort of Republicanism, the lightning might strike in 1944. Crystal-gazers who see a national "fusion" ticket winning in that year as city-wide fusion won in New York in 1933 and 1937 are far from ridiculous.

La Guardia himself says very little about his future hopes. But the unconcealed interest he displays when people talk about a third term for President Roosevelt has its own meaning. La Guardia is apparently quite convinced that Roosevelt won't be running this year, and third term talk has actually made him angry. Yet he has refused to show any real interest in Philip La

Follette's third party gestures—which are a long shot for 1944. Does this mean that La Guardia hopes to wangle something for himself on either the Republican or Democratic tickets this year? Ridiculous, you may say. But La Guardia has wangled things before, even in the face of united opposition. It is barely conceivable that he might end up this year as vice presidential candidate on a slate headed by an older—and frailer—man. Or he might "buy" himself a post as Secretary of Labor. He knows he has the implied veto power of a large personal following. And, as we have seen, he once got himself his seat in Congress by threatening to run for governor on an independent ticket. Is he contemplating getting himself a place on a national ticket by similar tactics? If William Allen White has his say, La Guardia will appear on the Republican national ticket. Bill White is admittedly not the Republican high command. But the American people are sniffing the breezes for political changes not comprehended by either Republicanism or Democracy, Old Style. And they are sniffing the breezes for something that is "different" from the New Deal. And La Guardia is sniffing the breezes, too.

At the Water's Edge

POLITICS, said Alf Landon in an all-too-quotable line, should stop at the water's edge. But the politics of stopping politics at the water's edge is something else again. It would be surprising indeed if there were ever to be agreement between Boston and Boise as to the strategic value of ten new battleships. Moreover, it would signify an unhealthy state of public opinion; the minute we begin to take our notions as to strategy, morality and commercial benefits from the same source it will be a sign that totalitarianism of the spirit is upon us. Between the Colorado sugar beet grower and the banker with an interest in Cuban cane fields and the consumer who wants cheap sugar there should be no easy compromise—for such compromise would mean death to the energies of man.

A nation's foreign policy is bound to reflect the divergencies as well as the uniformities in national opinion. In Britain, where most of the population can readily see the relationship between home production and world markets, or between home defense and the defense of overseas lifelines, the uniformities will naturally greatly overbalance the divergencies. In the United States, where few people are compelled to ponder upon the role (if any) which overseas commitments or entanglements play in their daily lives, the divergencies naturally outweigh the uniformities. The result, in our foreign policy, is confusion, even chaos. But a confused, contradictory and frequently impotent foreign policy is not necessarily a sign of national weakness. On the contrary, it may be a sign of strength: any nation blessed by geography and geology can afford to bicker over foreign policy. When United States citizens cease to fight over politics at the water's edge it will be an indication that doubt is upon us—the first portent of a coming rigor mortis in democracy. Let us thank God, therefore, that Standard Oil executives stationed in Venezuela and Mexican pecan-shellers living in Texas are still free to dispute the implications of the Good Neighbor policy. As long as there is argument on the surface there is bound to be democracy (in the Bill of Rights sense of the word) underneath.

Freedom to dissent, however, does not mean that individuals should cease to look for the basis of an intelligent foreign policy that will make room for personal, regional and occupational differences of opinion. Democratic politics rests on the assumption that areas of agreement can be reached by negotiation. Before the negotiation can be undertaken, however, there must be plenty of argument about the bases of a national military strategy, a national morality in foreign affairs, and a national design for economic life that will blend the maximum amount of cheapness (the international free trader's ideal) with the essential minimum of necessary security (the protectionist's demand). Little sense has been talked to date about our strategic, moral and economic interests for the simple reason that most of us begin with *a priori* philosophies, not with the relation of the American people to American geography. Free traders and protectionists are inclined to take all-or-nothing stands when arguing their points; democrats frequently assume as an article of faith that democracy and totalitarianism cannot exist side by side in the same world. As for the military men, they often confuse the institutional urge to growth that is part of any army and navy with the requirements of national defense.

Most people in the post-Marxian world of the Nineteen-thirties have ridden the economic interpretation pretty hard: they are accustomed to looking at foreign policy in the dollar diplomacy terms of overseas trade and investments. I cannot see that they are wholly right: if economic considerations were always the deciding factor our State Department would long ago have severed relations with Mexico over the oil expropriation dispute. Nor is imperialism always a matter of crude economic interest: our affection for the Monroe Doctrine is rooted partly in economics, partly in strategic considerations, but most of all in a desire to preserve a democratic form of government on the North American continent. The German and Japanese trade "menaces" in South America are and always have been negligible. But democracy doesn't thrive in an atmosphere of militarism—and strongly fortified German colonies to the south of us might conceivably impel us to counter with military measures that would undo our own democracy. It is for this simple reason that the man in the street has even more of a stake in the Monroe Doctrine than has the president of the International Business Machines Company. The man in the street will survive if no American comptometers are ever again sold in Rio. But if this hemisphere were to catch the habit of armed rivalries on a European scale then good-by to the blessed conditions under which college boys can laugh at the R.O.T.C. and drill sergeants can be regarded as a low form of animal life.

Having established a case for our own domestic moral interest in constraining the Venezuelans from presenting Europeans with air bases along the Caribbean, let me backtrack a bit. Nations often go to war for moral and strategic reasons. But a nation's morality and strategy are always related in some measure to its sources of livelihood. Woodrow Wilson could whip a whole nation up to the point of fighting in Flanders and the Argonne against a "menace" to our democratic way of life—the menace consisting of German domination of the "Atlantic" world. But who, beyond a few zealots, has ever been particularly exercised about the suppression of democratic aspirations in Afghanistan? Cordell Hull dislikes the "undemocratic" features of Nazi bilateral barter. But he has yet to condemn the barter system as practiced by the tribesmen of New Guinea.

A sensible foreign policy, then, must take account of moral and strategic factors only within certain limits: as C. Hartley Grattan has said, moral responsibility varies with proximity; and there is no sense in maintaining military strongholds—say in Guam or the Philippines—that will cost more than they are worth to defend. But what are the limits which ought to circumscribe a sensible U. S. foreign policy? Are there points at which the U. S. should fight over trade conditions in Europe, Africa or the Orient? "Internationalists" say yes; "isolationists" say no. And both have their say on the subject with considerable emotion. Neither side has ever stopped to reflect on the possibility that the U. S. doesn't have to bother to say anything at all. A configurative analysis of the relation of the U. S. economy to the rest of the world leads inevitably to a philosophy of economic indifference. By this I do not mean the indifference of apathy. I mean the indifference of the poker player whose hand consists of four legitimate aces and a deuce in a game in which the deuces are wild. Stephen Leacock once said: "The Americans don't give a damn; don't need to—never did need to. That is their salvation." The words certainly do not apply to America's domestic problems. But they still more or less apply so far as our economic relations with the rest of the world are concerned. With the possible exception of Russia, we are the only nation in the world that could afford the self-sufficiency of autarchy. But by the same token we don't need autarchy; we can have both peace and trade. Of all the nations on the surface of the earth, the U. S. is in a seller's market. Which means that we can specify our conditions without having to fight for them.

Early in 1939, testifying before a Senate committee that seemed impressed with the desirability of slapping an increased duty on imported vegetable oils, Assistant Secretary of State Francis B. Sayre pleaded long and eloquently for the free-trade position. His words were as winged with hope and idealism as ever were those of Richard Cobden and John Bright, the classical mid-nineteenth century crusaders for a world without tariffs, quotas, and exchange restrictions. If only, so Mr. Sayre argued in effect, if only all the nations would put their signatures to reciprocal trade pacts shaped up by Cordell Hull, then we might possibly look forward to recovering some of our lost overseas markets for cotton and wheat. But if the honorable senators—and some of them were Southern senators, at that—insisted on increasing the tax on imported vegetable fats, then how could you expect Britishers, for example, to prefer Carolina cotton to the Indian variety? There was no answer in logic to Mr. Sayre's words; his victory was positively brilliant.

Early in 1939 Stuart Chase wrote a pamphleteering book called "The New Western Front." If, so he argued, if some genie were to throw an electrified fence round the U. S., thus cutting off all exports and imports, the results would not prove fatal; we could carry on. Moreover, from any long-term point of view, it might be better if the genie were to conjure up the high-voltage barrier: the resultant self-sufficiency would enable us to dispense with the need to fight in other folks' wars; we could give up notions of policing the planet. Given the triumphs of industrial chemistry, of advanced metallurgy and of agro-biology, the U. S. and its natural sphere of economic influence in the Caribbean area and northern South America could achieve plenty on an autarchic basis in a very few years. Substitutes for raw silk, for natural rubber, for the older ferro-alloys, are being discovered or improved every day; wool can be spun from milk, "gasoline" can be made from wood or cane sugar, steering wheels can be fashioned out of soy beans, and nitrate fertilizers can be purloined from the air. As David Cushman Coyle says, anything can be made of anything else. There was no answer in logic to Mr. Chase's words; his victory was positively brilliant.

But, as Senator La Follette said after listening to Mr. Sayre testify, you can't "if" your way to prosperity. Both Mr. Sayre and Stuart Chase are "if" men who build visions of a better world (or a more independent United States) on the highly insecure foundations of purely rhetorical supposition. Mr. Sayre's supposition is that six or seven great powers, no two of which are equal in raw resources, industrial development, money, or geographical position, can achieve the common will that is a prerequisite for an internationalist world. Mr. Chase's supposition is that a genie-electrician might, somehow, prove more powerful than the cotton senators and the wheat senators. Of the two suppositions, it is a toss-up as to which is the more unreal.

Both Mr. Sayre and Mr. Chase are guilty of a common error of publicists in assuming that a nation's interests must be "pure," or logically self-consistent, or all-of-a-piece. Actually, the "national interest" of which our publicists and statesmen prate cannot in the nature of things be satisfactory to any philosopher in search of verbal consistency, for it is a blend, a composite, of a hundred group regional and class interests. As such, it must be a ragged, even an amorphous, working compromise, a bit of Idaho here, a touch of Joe Grundy protectionism there, a bit of Cotton Ed Smith's Carolina countryside added to flavor the whole. When the working compromise is reduced to paper it is bound to seem intellectually stultifying, even nonsensical. But the "nonsense" derives not from the world of reality but from the human propensity to think in terms of polar abstractions.

In the world of reality it is a fact that our exports account for only five per cent of our annual national income. This contrasts markedly with the British figure of twenty per cent, or the French of twenty-five. In other words, the U. S. economy is more than ninety per cent self-contained. But this neither means that we shall push on to one hundred per cent autarchy nor go in the English direction. It is pretty safe to predict that the United States of the future is not going to be vastly different from the United States of the past twenty years so far as its position in world commerce is concerned. We may go to war for any number of reasons; but in the long run we are certain to revert to a position that is a mixture of "internationalism" and "isolationism," with the latter predominating for the purely material reason that more than ninety per cent of our national income is generated from exploitation of the home market. Yet, although the home market vastly overshadows our markets overseas, we shall probably follow lines of least resistance and trade and lend abroad to the extent that we do already.

Such a conclusion is not exciting; it cannot result in the recruiting of schools and counter-schools, it cannot array the Chases against the Sayres. But it is the only possible conclusion that can be drawn from realistic analysis of the U. S. as a trading and lending nation. It suggests, as a corollary, that we put the internationalist-isolationist squabble in its proper perspective down at the bottom of the list of "burning questions." Mr. Hull's efforts to knock down barriers to trade by his campaign for reciprocity are all very worthy; but success along these lines is not going to revive an economy that does ninety per cent of its business at home. On the other hand, a nation that is more than ninety per cent self-sufficient can afford the luxury of being ten per cent "internationalist" without fears of "encircle-ment" or of *necessarily* being drawn into other peoples' wars.

With a humanitarian in the White House and lesser humanitarians running the State Department we are not of course apt to formulate policy on any basis of pure realism. Yet the United States could, if it chose to do so, adopt a take-it-or-leave-it attitude that would enable it to have the best of both the internationalist and isolationist worlds. A nation that normally sells abroad only enough goods to account for five per cent of the annual national income will be vexed, even pro-foundly disturbed in certain areas, by warfare that dis-rupts sea-borne commerce; but the trouble would not prove fatal. For that matter, export trade would still continue, breaking out in new places; it always does. Conversely, a nation that buys annually some $3,000,-000,000 worth of foreign goods—which is a prodigious amount as import figures are reckoned—is not apt to go without needed materials; importing persists even in the most unlikely circumstances, and there is no way to blockade an entire continent. Japan's war in China has resulted in disturbances in the tungsten, antimony, tung oil, green tea, and North China pig bristle markets, yet none of this has hurt many Americans. True, the price of tungsten and green tea and pig bristles has risen. But companies like Westinghouse Electric keep a ten-year supply of tungsten ore on hand, green tea is a luxury, and there are chemical substitutes for pig bristles, as Du Pont can tell you. As for tung oil, they are now raising tung trees in Mississippi. Certain groups are always hit by other peoples' wars, but the loss can never be commensurate with the loss to the American nation as a whole should it engage in a war to preserve the classic freedom of the seas. And it must be remembered that when certain groups are hit by martial dislocation other groups gain. On balance, there is compensation, as the war-born American chemical industry can testify.

The more jittery of the God's-sake school is concerned with the permanent effects of war; they frequently argue that "aggressor" nations might cut us off forever from needed raw materials. Specifically, they have in mind our sources of rubber and tin in the British and Dutch East Indies. Now there may be any number of good cases to be made out for continued white rule of the Malay Archipelago. But none of these cases is worth very much from a long-term economic standpoint. For no matter who controls the East Indies, neither the rubber nor the tin—especially in this age of *ersatz*—is going to be worth very much to their exploiters unless it can be sold to the nation which has led the world in the making and marketing of automobile tires and canned goods. The United States is the most prodigious market for other peoples' raw materials that the world has ever seen: it has the whip hand of the consumer whose purse is filled (with half the world's gold supply) and whose own raw materials are so copious that only a modicum of ingenuity would be required to provide substitutes for any overseas commodities. Whether Japan or Holland or Britain "owns" the East Indies, the mine and plantation owners of that part of the world must sell in Akron or Pittsburgh or else face prolonged depression. I am aware that this argument is not likely to prove popular; most Americans, including myself, would like to see Japan fall flat on its ugly aggressor's face. But if you don't believe it is a valid argument, take a look at Japan as a producer of raw silk. The "menacing" Japanese have a practical corner on the world's silk worms, but they have never seen fit to withhold raw silk from our markets. Indeed, the shoe is on the other foot: Japan is scared stiff lest the Du Ponts and Celanese Corporation cut her silk exporters out of the American market with their new synthetic fibers.

It is not part of my intention here to cram the case for a take-it-or-leave-it attitude toward Europe and Asia down anyone's throat. The case must be documented, it must spring naturally from an analysis of the U. S. position in the world, to be convincing. Such an analysis should proceed in two dimensions: that of historical time and that of types of commodities bought and sold today. Analysis in the time-dimension should demonstrate, roughly, just what is solid and what is illusory in our hopes for certain great staples as they enter international trade. And analysis of what is bought and sold as of this decade ought to prove something about the basic needs of our modern, mass-production economy.

First, as to the dimension of time. The U. S. began as an exporter of raw materials and foodstuffs; classically, our interest in overseas markets has involved two great regions of our economy, the cotton region and the wheat region. Cotton is still our most important export commodity; more than half of what we raise is for sale abroad, and in 1936 this one item accounted for fifteen per cent of all our exports. But, year by year, our cotton market has been shaved away, willy-nilly. The 1924-33 ten-year export average was approximately 8,000,000 bales; by 1937 exports had fallen to 5,700,-000 bales. Meanwhile, Brazil, North China, India, Egypt, Turkey, and Russia were upping their acreage; world production outside the U. S. jumped from 14,-000,000 bales to 19,000,000 in a five-year span. Since other nations can produce cotton more cheaply than the worn-out eastern areas of the American South, there is no good reason to suppose that this particular trend will be reversed. When perfected, the Rust mechanical cotton picker might cut our costs of production, but the Rust picker can be used elsewhere, and, anyway, the problem of unemployed share-croppers would cancel the trade gains due to technological improvement in cotton production. Hence a war to preserve our "fair" share of the world's cotton market—say, a war to prevent Japan from shifting its cotton purchases from Houston, Texas, to North China—promises no permanent balm; the problem of the one-crop American South is chronic, and must be solved on some other basis than the attempted re-coronation of King Cotton by *force majeure*.

Similarly with wheat, which we have been "dumping" abroad through the medium of the Federal Surplus Commodities Corporation. The story of how Americans carried wheat farming into the Dust Bowl in the war years is an old one; farm land values and mortgages were fixed in those years on the basis of an unhealthy war trade that took no account of the obvious fact that eastern European grain lands would come back into production with the cessation of hostilities. Excluding Russia and China, world wheat production rose from an average of 3,000,000,000 bushels before the War to 3,700,000,000 in the early 1930's; and it is Utopian to suppose that the American wheat grower can ever recapture his one-time dominant position in the world's markets.

Two simple tables tell the story of the shift in America's import-export position better than multitudes of words. The first is for 1821 as contrasted with 1933:

EXPORT PERCENTAGES

	Crude materials and foodstuffs	Manufactures
1821	84.92	15.08
1933	48.17	51.83

IMPORT PERCENTAGES

| 1821 | 35.66 | 64.34 |
| 1933 | 57.63 | 42.37 |

The second table, published by the U. S. Department of Commerce, divides our foreign trade into five economic classes:

Class	1936	1937
(figures in millions of dollars)		

Exports of U. S. merchandise:

	1936	1937
Crude materials	668	722
Crude foodstuffs	58	102
Manufactured foodstuffs	144	177
Semi-manufactures	395	677
Finished manufactures	1,154	1,617

Imports for consumption:

	1936	1937
Crude materials	733	974
Crude foodstuffs	349	413
Manufactured foodstuffs	386	440
Semi-manufactures	490	634
Finished manufactures	466	551

Keep these figures in mind; two-thirds of our exports are today in manufactured goods (as compared to a mere 15 per cent for 1821), whereas two-thirds of our modern imports are of raw materials and foodstuffs. The agricultural stake in foreign trade is diminishing; moreover, the agricultural regions are today turning protectionist in their philosophy. The duty on butter is fourteen cents a pound, that on meat is six cents a pound, shelled filberts are protected by a duty of 51 per cent of the value, shelled walnuts are protected to the tune of 101 per cent. Poultry is one of our great protected industries and it is not so "infant." The significance of this growth of rural Hamiltonianism will become apparent later on; meanwhile, let us analyze our foreign trade from the regional standpoint, showing exactly where we buy and sell.

Regionally, our greatest customer is the continent of Europe, which in 1937 * took $1,355,700,000—or about two-fifths—of our total exports of $3,345,200,000. Of the European total, $534,600,000 went to the United Kingdom, our biggest customer among the nations. Canada, second largest individual customer of the U. S., bought $509,500,000 worth of our goods—which is natural, for Canada is part of the regional economy of North America. The third country in the U. S. export trade is Japan, which spent $288,400,000 in the U. S. in 1937. This figure is about "normal" for our Japanese market; for as the Japanese cut down on their purchases of American cotton they have increased their purchases of scrap iron, copper, and petroleum to balance their own exports to the U. S. of raw silk, crabmeat, dolls, and silk fabrics. The entire continent of Asia absorbed only $579,000,000 worth of American goods in 1937. South America, which figures in the imaginations of this generation of exporters as the

* I use 1937 figures because they are the last to give even a relatively true picture of trade realities in a peacetime world.

"China market" figured in the generation of John Hay, accounted for a paltry $318,400,000—or less than France, Germany, and Italy combined. The Australian and African markets were negligible.

But if Europe is our greatest customer, it is not our biggest supplier. We took $843,600,000 in imports from Europe in 1937 as compared to $967,400,000 from Asia. Canada, which comes first on the list as an individual source of American imports, sold us $398,-500,000 worth of goods. Our grand import total for the year was $3,084,100,000. Unlike Germany, which is a nation without monetary resources, we have never been faced with the necessity of balancing our trade bilaterally; most of our purchases are in the seventy per cent segment of the world's economy that is still "free" —i.e., that still uses an international money system which enables it to triangulate its sales and purchases. The triangulation works simply. For example, we sell to the United Kingdom almost twice as much as we buy from her. But our purchases from Brazil are almost double our exports to Brazil. Some of the excess American foreign exchange which Brazil gets from us goes to Britain, and Britain, in turn, sends it back to the U. S. for Iowa pork products. Again, our purchases from British Malaya are $235,200,000 as compared with $8,800,000 exports to Singapore. Presumably, the fact that we buy more from British Malaya and sell more to the British Isles helps to balance the empire's accounts.

The American Stakes

Superficially considered, a contemplation of the import-export figures would lead to this conclusion: our "national interest" demands the perpetuation of the British Empire. The United Kingdom and Canada together absorb a third of our exports; while our crucial raw materials—primarily nickel, rubber, and tin—come from Canada, British Malaya, and the Dutch East Indies, with the last two regions dependent on the British Navy and Singapore Base for safety. Our "interests" would also seem to demand the promotion of our industrial exports. For, although the rest of the world is doing its best to make itself independent of our cotton and our wheat, it still has need of our high-grade machine tools, our strip mill machinery, our mass-produced automobiles, our typewriters and adding machines, and our tractors and combines.

So defined, our "national interest" must express itself in terms of "parallel" diplomatic action with Great Britain, plus a competitive peddling of our superior industrial exports as against Germany's inferior brand. In other words, Herbert Hoover's foreign policy was the correct one. But was it? I presume to doubt it. No mere analysis of the isolate facts of our foreign trade is sufficient to form a basis for foreign policy; there must, first of all, be a *configurative* analysis of the U. S. economy as a whole. The relationships of the foreign-trade figures to the annual national income of 130,000,000 people must be indicated; and the profits from overseas purchases and sales must be balanced against the costs of maintaining a military and naval establishment sufficient to indulge in "parallel" or "collective" action that might lead to war in Far Eastern waters or in European trenches.

I have already indicated that "ownership" of tropical rubber and tin is immaterial to us in the long run; an economy that does sixty or seventy billion dollars' worth of business a year is going to have salesmen on its doorstep no matter what the nationality. Our need to maintain the British Empire for trade reasons (as opposed to moral or strategic reasons) is largely illusory; and as we shall see a Germanized Europe without military and naval and air bases near our shores could hardly menace us any more than we could menace a united Europe. Moreover, should Britain collapse, Canada, Newfoundland, Jamaica, and other British possessions in North America would fall immediately into the U. S. sphere of influence. The Canadian trade would not only continue, it would even increase. As for the forcing of exports, there are, theoretically, two ways of doing it. One way is to reduce our tariffs, thus enabling foreigners to sell their goods in our markets for dollars that can be translated into purchases of U. S. automobiles and office equipment. The other way is to lend money—i.e., make U. S. dollar exchange credits available—abroad.

Tariff reduction has much to commend it; the Hawley-Smoot rates are ridiculous and Cordell Hull's reciprocal trade treaties are simple common sense. Low tariffs have this beneficial effect: they mean a non-monopolistic price structure at home. Yet it is to be doubted whether tariff reduction on industrial goods would vastly increase the markets for our own industrial products abroad. A good deal of balderdash has been written about "the American way" in industry. But there is a hard core of reality to the balderdash: with a nation of 130,000,000 consumers spread over a continental area, we have been able to afford the mass-production experimentation that has resulted in the super-efficiency of Detroit. (Mass production is a reflex of the American road system, which is not duplicated elsewhere in the world.) The automobile industry, which takes a low-unit but big overall profit, is not a "protected" industry. Yet it pays the highest wages in the world. With cheaper labor, it costs the British three times as much as Detroit to make and market an automobile. Where tariffs and quotas do not interfere, our automobiles naturally undersell all others in export markets. American efficiency and technological superiority extend to other things, thus making the "menace" of "cheap" foreign labor a politician's illusion. It is the hourly productiveness, not the individual labor-hour cost, that is the important item when we come to figure wage bills. For example, American shoe factories produce 1,650 pairs of shoes per worker per year in contrast to British production of 1,003 pairs. Japanese labor is ridiculously low on an hourly wage basis, but go over to Bloomfield or to Newark, N. J., and watch the complicated Westinghouse Electric and General Electric light-bulb machinery at work. With this super-ingenious mechanical aid, high-wage workers are able to produce so many electric light bulbs per man per hour that Japanese competition is no longer a bogy. Where unit labor costs are high—as in the manufacture of heavy electrical machinery—the same rule doesn't hold. But even here we do not need to worry about the "flooding" of our markets; neither England nor Germany has the physical plant nor the available man-power to demoralize our markets with heavy stuff. Given universal free trade, our textile industry might suffer. But here too we are as clever as the next nation: modernization of our plant with the latest thing in electrical spinning buckets should make the labor differential less important. In general, our manufacturers are fixed to hold the home market even without tariff protection. Tariff reduction would result in lower prices; but Detroit and Pittsburgh would still be collecting the consumers' dollars.

With our manufacturers keeping a solid grip on the home market, American imports would still consist largely of crude rubber, tin, manganese, nickel, jute, coffee, cane sugar, cocoanut oil, cacao, tropical fruits, raw silk, furs, and specialty products such as Belgian laces, Irish oatmeal, and Canadian lacrosse sticks. (I eliminate copper and oil, for our "imports" of these products are largely from American-owned mines and wells in Chile, Venezuela, and elsewhere, which means that we are paying foreign exchange into our own pockets except for wages involved.) It is the quantum of dollar exchange that we shake loose into the outside world for raw materials and tropical foodstuffs that largely determines what foreigners will spend in our markets for our automobiles and trucks, our petroleum products, our office equipment. And there is apparently no sound way of shaking large blocks of dollar exchange loose except in the normal processes of buying raw materials and tropical produce which we do not have at home.

Here the "internationalist" will argue that we could lend money abroad and so create a market for our goods. But the argument that we can profitably shake dollar exchange loose in large amounts by a revival of foreign lending is, on the face of it, specious. For lending, if it is not to go sour on us as it did in the early 1930's, must be for economic purposes; it must result in production-for-sale, or else both debt service and principal repayments will prove unmanageable. (Our war loans collapsed for the obvious reason that they were blown away into the air of No Man's Land in France.) Moreover, the sale must be made, ultimately, on American soil, for debt and interest payments are acceptable to U. S. citizens only in dollars. But if American manufacturers continue to hold the home market for the big industrial items, foreign industrial borrowers will not be able to put their hands on dollar

exchange for interest and amortization. We must buy
in bulk from abroad if we are to lend money abroad;
and there is no good reason to suppose that our import
habits are going to change drastically in the next
decade. Gold of course is still acceptable to us—but
with half the world's gold already buried in Kentucky,
foreigners outside of the gold-mine-owning British
Empire are going to find it increasingly difficult to
purchase dollar exchange with the precious metal.
Given peace, our tourists would, naturally, continue to
shake dollar exchange loose in Paris and London; and
immigrants will continue to send U. S. coin back to the
home country. But tourist expenditures and immigrant
remittances and money spent for shipping charges are
not apt to be large in a world of war preparations, im-
migration quotas, and autarchic urges.

There remains one alternative possibility of shaking
loose the dollar exchange needed to finance a growing
export trade. And that possibility involves, in Louis
Hacker's words, the "doom" of the American farmer:
we could, if we were so disposed, balance the export of
industrial goods by importing large quantities of Ar-
gentine beef, Australian wheat, Polish pork, New
Zealand and Danish dairy products, even Brazilian
cotton. When England repealed her grain tariffs in the
1840's she took just such a course. But the U. S. is a
continental area, not an island, and its farm population
is politically intrenched. Ask Charlie Holman, secretary of the Dairymen's Association, if he is prepared to

pay for the export of American automobiles with imports of New Zealand or Danish butter. I have already indicated that rural Hamiltonianism is growing; and with one-half the voting population living in farm areas it is not likely that the trend will be reversed. Nor should it be reversed; the farmer is an incurable democrat, and he should be kept alive even by an uneconomic tariff if we wish to preserve a republican form of government.

Look back at our tables, at the heavy import preponderance of crude materials and of foodstuffs that are largely tropical in origin. In that preponderance lies the inevitable key to America's foreign trade future. Why do raw materials bulk so large in our imports? For one reason: the vastness, the richness, of the U. S. home market which requires a certain proportion of foreign materials in the manufactures produced for 130,000,000 people. If we are making lots of cars, our rubber needs will jump correspondingly. If 130,000,-000 Americans are filling their bellies, tin purchases for canning purposes will be correspondingly huge. And with dollar exchange going abroad for raw materials, our exports will also swing upward in a reciprocal relationship that has been maintained ever since the end of the World War. When the annual national income is $80,000,000,000, we buy some four billion dollars' worth of goods abroad and sell just short of five billion (the difference being made up in foreign loans). When the national income drops to $40,000,-000,000, our purchases in foreign markets fall to a billion-and-a-half, and our export sales are short of two billion. The conclusion, while it is admittedly a matter of empirical assumption rather than mathematical proof, would seem to be obvious: the only way to increase our export trade is, first of all, to increase the total exchange of goods and services at home.

The tail of the export trade might, conceivably, wag the dog of the U. S. home economy; such, at any rate, is Secretary of State Cordell Hull's assumption. But how much easier it is for a dog to wag a tail! Widen the home market and you automatically increase imports. Increase imports and you shake dollar exchange loose on the world. Shake dollar exchange loose and people will spend it for your goods; it is no good to them otherwise. The circle is complete; and a wise domestic policy becomes, *ipso facto*, the only sort of foreign trade policy we should pursue. Let Mr. Hull push his reciprocal trade pacts. But, for heaven's sake, don't let's substitute the Hull policy for a concern with the more homely matters of wages, prices, and production within the confines of the forty-eight states of the U. S. A. If we don't expand the home market Mr. Hull won't be around very long to initial his treaties with Venezuela, Turkey, and the noble kingdom of Ruritania. We must look inward if we are to look outward: such is the paradox of our peculiar position as a continental market in a world of petty states.

The American Stakes

It should be agreed, then, that the U. S. doesn't have to fight for trade; it will continue to get what it wants because it is a great natural customer, and it will continue to sell up to the limit of its ability to shake loose dollar exchange in the rest of the world. If it must continue to pay monopoly prices for raw rubber and tin to the so-called "free trade" nations of Britain and Holland, it will cheerfully do so up to a point. Beyond that point, however, it will go in for Du Pont's synthetic rubber and cellulose containers for canned foods. It will take manganese, an essential to the steel industry, from Soviet Russia—but should the "freedom of the seas" be blocked it will make shift with Cuban or Brazilian manganese ores. And, by virtue of the Webb-Pomerene Act, which exempts foreign traders from the anti-trust law, American exporters will take their own monopoly toll of world trade in the fields where international cartels control prices. None of this adds up to the world-picture of the free-traders Cobden and Bright, but a nation that does ninety per cent of its business at home can afford to forego the bloody attempt to establish an international free trader's Utopia. A world of conflicting sovereignties, of differing price levels, of unequal allocation of gold deposits, of a hundred and fifty widely varying standards of culture, isn't going to submit tamely to Cobdenization by fiat from Geneva; and the alternative is a combined U. S.-British police program that would cost more immediately in terms of naval tonnage and military up-

170

keep than individuals would gain in a century from reductions in the cost of living. Mr. Hull's reciprocal trade program, provided it can escape protectionist hatchet men in Congress, may limber up the system a bit here and there; but it is a dead cinch that war, which impoverishes all countries and makes for more rigid economic "controls" everywhere, will not contribute to the limbering process in even the slightest degree.

If a war for trade or freedom of the seas promises nothing, however, it still remains true that the U. S. should be sufficiently well armed to protect its western hemisphere territory, its Caribbean-Panama communications, and its political system, from the designs of any marauders. But what armaments are "enough"? With the "experts" differing radically among themselves, laymen are frequently informed they have no business invading such a thorny field of controversy. Yet laymen—through their representatives in Congress —have to choose among the "experts." Moreover, there are certain underlying truths which military and naval men, with their natural institutional urge to expand their organizations, are apt to forget.

Even in the sanguinary event of a totalitarian conquest of Europe, the trembling of the patriots would be misplaced. Back in 1937 (which seems aeons ago) Mauritz Hallgren asked himself a pertinent question in a first-rate and completely forgotten book called "The Tragic Fallacy." It must be asked, said Mr.

Hallgren, "what a foreign power or combination of powers would hope to gain by conquering the U. S." A victorious Prussian conqueror could hardly hope to sit forever over the 130,000,000 bankers, manufacturers, workers and farmers of a country 3,000 miles wide, compelling them to work for a master race of 80,000,-000 Germans who were at the same time busy policing disaffected Frenchmen, Britons, Dutchmen, Danes, Poles, Czechs, Hungarians and Jews. True, the victorious conqueror might hope to seize America's gold. But whoever supposes that the gold would stay put in its Kentucky hole in the event of impending defeat? Wouldn't a nation about to capitulate first dump its gold into the waters of the Pacific? The victor, of course, could demand reparations. The post-Versailles history of Germany, however, is pretty good evidence that reparations are impossible to collect. They cannot be taken in the form of goods and services, for the home producers object to the competition. And they cannot be collected in paper currency, for such currency is useless inside the collecting country. If they are to be collected in gold, they imply a continued use of force to ensure the annual payment. But again we come back to the difficulty of policing 130,000,000 people over a period long enough to wring big reparations out of gold mines as far apart as Georgia and Alaska.

Attempts to picture a foreign invasion of the modern United States, a nation with fifty per cent of the world's steel capacity, must inevitably run out into lurid fantasy. Still, insanity is a fact of nature; and we may assume for the sake of argument that an all-European dictator might be crazy enough to try to overrun and conquer an empire that reaches from Penobscot Bay to beyond Death Valley.

The mad dictator must, first of all, beat us to the gun in seizing supporting sea bases in the Azores and Bermuda—an unlikely event in view of America's bumptiousness when actually menaced. Even assuming he could grab the Azores ahead of us, the dictator must then sail west for a thousand and more miles before he can engage the United States fleet, which is second only to Britain's and superior to the combined fleets of Germany, Italy and Japan. Now it may be granted that I know little about naval strategy. But it seems obvious that the American fleet could take its stand at a point where it would benefit from full support of the aerial arm working from shore landing fields. Moreover, the invading fleet would be working far from bases of supply—and its lines of communication would for many miles be open to attack both from the air and from under the sea. Back in 1916 Admiral Knight told a House of Representatives Naval Committee that "a fleet going out there [to Japan] would be accompanied, necessarily, by a tremendous attendant fleet, a train . . . of auxiliary ammunition ships, hospital ships, and so forth. The problem of conducting such a train as that in going thousands of miles through hostile waters is probably the most serious problem that could possibly be put to a commander-in-chief." The Pacific is wider than the Atlantic, of course. But modern technology, instead of increasing the attacking radius of navies, actually works to diminish it. It is axiomatic that a frigate could pick its motive power from the four winds where a modern battleship must stop to refuel. But even beyond this, battleships must be chary of venturing far from home base and close to distant enemy coasts. Inasmuch as the effective bombing radius of the airplane flying in formation is only 750 or at most 1,000 miles, the U. S. is not menaced by European air armadas. But an enemy fleet that came within 1,000 miles of Long Island would be menaced by our air armada to an extent that Admiral Knight could never have known in 1916. The good Admiral's words are, then, even truer today than when they were originally uttered.

But since we are playing "let's pretend," let us push our fantasy even to the limits of an Edgar Rice Burroughs thriller. Let us assume the dictator has swept the Atlantic of all opposing first-line ships. Let us assume the way is open for great convoys of troops. Then, surely, the patriots must tremble.

First of all, however, the invading dictator must have a fleet of transports for his army: it takes twelve-and-one-half tons of merchant ship to transport and provision a single soldier. Germany, Italy and Japan have no merchant fleets sufficiently large to carry even a middling-respectable army of, say, 400,000. But for purposes of argument, we may assume the dictator has possessed himself of Dutch, Danish, French and British cargo boats. Then, surely, he could get an impressive army across the Atlantic, through fog, wind and wave.

Well, he could—given time. But what troubles he would have! Looking back over U. S. experience in the World War, Mauritz Hallgren notes that it took seventeen months to carry the A.E.F. to France. The movement of troops began in June of 1917. In December only 50,000 men were transported; by the following April we were moving a monthly total of 120,000. In May the total jumped to 245,000; in June of 1918 the number was 280,000. The peak month, July, saw 305,000 doughboys crossing the water.

These figures are impressive. But to accomplish our great troop movements, we had to impress captured German ships and charter considerable chunks of Dutch, Scandinavian and Japanese tonnage. Moreover, we had to strain ourselves to the utmost to build a million tons of new ships of our own. Eventually, by dint of begging, borrowing, building and stealing ships all over the world, we got together some 3,800,000 tons. But according to Mr. Hallgren, even this prodigious fleet could do no better than move 305,000 soldiers to France in any one month. The record in moving supplies was much less impressive: where it took 400,-000 tons of shipping to move 305,000 men, it required 1,350,000 tons to carry equipment and provisions in the same month. General Sherman's army could live off the country, but a modern army must carry tons and tons of tanks, howitzers, motor vehicles, machine guns, ambulances, small arms, ammunition, field telephone equipment, shovels, concrete mixers, airplanes, oil, gasoline, and food.

So far, we have been giving the dictator the breaks by setting up an analogy that cannot be pushed to the close. For, unlike the U. S. in 1917, the dictator would have Frenchmen, Britons, Poles, Hungarians and Czechs waiting to stab him in the back at home. And in 1917 the U. S. sailed its expeditionary force into friendly harbors and landed miles behind the line of fire. A dictator invading the U. S. would, of course, be compelled to land on intensely hostile shores. Should he elect to force a landing in any deep water harbor, say Boston or New York, he would first have to pulverize our coast defense batteries. And presumably his landing operations would have to be carried on under heavy bombing attack from U. S. airplanes. The history of the Dardanelles campaign in the first World War should be sufficient to dissuade even the maddest Napoleon from attempting to disembark large numbers of troops on a fortified or defended coast. Theoretically, the invader might try to land at some unfortified inlet. But it would be a sluggish U. S. indeed if our war department were to permit any deep-water inlets to go unmined in time of threatening invasion.

Even assuming the worst, even assuming the successful landing of the hostile army, what then? The hostile army would, as Mr. Hallgren remarks, be thousands of miles from home in a hostile foreign land—a small force of limited strength, dependent upon the equipment and supplies it had brought with it. It would be facing a nation of continental proportions, a huge nation with a small but effective army of its own. Even should it defeat that army, it would be hard put to it to seize and hold *all* the strategic points—New York, Connecticut's Naugatuck Valley, Pittsburgh, Detroit, the wheat lands of the northwestern plains, the mines of Minnesota and Alabama. The invading army would be a mere globule of ink attempting to black out an enormous blotter. It would be—but why go on with this fantastic nonsense? As Stuart Chase has said, the topic is an admirable one for discussion in a lunatic asylum.

We are told, however, that the world is "closer together" these days. We are told that a sea blockade might cause a delicately adjusted industrial mechanism to collapse, that Canada might surrender to a European conqueror, that an aerial "egg" laid on one of the locks of the Panama Canal might seriously disrupt both our defense and our economy, that Japan might make a successful grab for the Philippines (our one really vulnerable outpost), that our South American trade might be stolen by native totalitarian revolutionaries working in cahoots with a European nation to make an end of the Monroe Doctrine. All of these threats are, to some degree, actual; and we must take steps to meet them. But only one is ever likely to prove serious: a Japanese attempt to achieve hegemony of the Philippines.

Let us consider the threats in the order of their importance to the American people. A blockade would indeed cause us trouble—but even the combined British, French, German, Italian and Japanese battlefleets would be hard put to it to close all our Atlantic, Gulf coast and Pacific ports.

Let us assume the worst again: let us assume that we have lost command of the deep-water lanes of the Atlantic and Pacific. What would this mean to the U. S. economy? During the War of 1812 a blockade of our big eastern ports raised the devil with the internal economy of the young U. S. for the simple reason that we depended then on sea-borne coastal commerce for interchange of our own products. Today, however, our automobile highways and our railroad system and our oil pipelines give us full command of necessary internal transport. From this standpoint, we are much less vulnerable than we were in the days of Mr. Madison.

As for critical and strategic raw materials, a successful blockade would cause a good deal of trouble. But, with the passages of the West Indies protected, our Gulf of Mexico-Caribbean commerce with northern South America would almost certainly continue. We could still have Colombian and Guatemalan coffee; sisal from

Yucatan; tropic vegetable oils, bananas, Cuban manganese, Cuban cane sugar. It is misleading, therefore, to complain that our truly important list of critical and strategic raw materials includes coffee, sisal, vegetable oils, bananas, manganese and cane sugar, for the Caribbean region is as much "ours" as is Texas. Rubber, silk, tin, tungsten, antimony, nickel and nitrates are more serious matters. The nitrates, however, can be taken from the air that bathes every inch of the continental U. S. Nickel comes from neighborly Canada. The U. S. has tungsten and antimony deposits, as well as some manganese. It may cost more to work these deposits, but in war we have to be prepared to pay the cost. Rubber, silk and tin remain to be considered. Three or four years ago any blockade of the trade routes leading to the East Indies and Japan, chief sources of these products, would have caused mighty headaches in the U. S. But today?

Here is where the much-derided "ersatz," or substitute, chemistry comes in to save the day. The Du Ponts are now making a synthetic rubber at four times the cost of raw rubber from the East Indies; this rubber may not stand friction as well as the natural product, but the Germans have been getting along on their own variant of it, and no doubt we could make a fair shift with it, too. Once mass production methods are applied to the making of synthetic rubber, the costs will come way down. Moreover, we could by some foresighted planting increase the supply of raw rubber

179

we are now getting from the Caribbean region and South America. Admitting that the outer Atlantic lane to Brazilian ports on the Amazon could be closed, it might prove practicable in time of war to float raw rubber down the Orinoco tributaries into Venezuela and bring it to Houston, Texas, through the Caribbean. Raw rubber might even be grown in the U. S.—at least I have heard Texans claim that rubber trees can thrive in the lower Rio Grande Valley.

Raw silk, of which we normally import a hundred million dollars' worth annually, would have been a problem even a year ago. But it is no problem at all at the moment, for the Du Ponts are already marketing their nylon hosiery, made out of a base of coal, water and air. Unlike rayon, nylon has qualities that make it indistinguishable from silk so far as appearance is concerned. And its durability is much greater than that of silk. To dramatize the toughness of nylon thread, girls have paraded up and down beaches in their stocking feet for hours without wearing holes in the fabric.

As for tin, our prime use of that metal is for coating "tin" cans. Women like tin-coated cans, for they look clean. But lacquer coating is just as practicable, and aluminum cans can be manufactured out of home-ground bauxite if necessary. For that matter, food can be put up in containers made out of cellulose: the Germans used 133,000,000 cellulose "cans" in 1938 as substitutes for tinned steel.

A deep-water blockade, then, is hardly likely to prove fatal: the 130,000,000 people of the U. S. could still live on, although something would have to be done to support cotton and wheat farmers through a period of drastic readjustment. The threats to South America, to Canada, to the Panama Canal, are all more serious: here, if we want to put teeth in the Monroe Doctrine, we must be prepared to help needy economies to the south of us, to insist on our right to air-bases in Newfoundland and Trinidad should Britain collapse as an empire, and to keep our fleet and our Caribbean and Hawaiian bases up to snuff. As for the Philippines they are a liability both economically and strategically; they would cost a national fortune to defend in a cross-ocean war with Japan, for Japan actually lies *between* Manila and the North American continent on the great circle ship route. For years the disciples of John Hay of Open Door fame hoped the Philippines would serve as our lever to pry open the "China market." But somehow the Chinese coolies never managed to get hold of the requisite purchasing power to buy our cotton shirts. With the China market a lost dream of a lost time, the economic motive for hanging on to the Philippines is wholly lacking. True, we have a moral commitment to the Filipinos: we cannot leave them to their fate even though they are to be granted complete independence. But there is no reason why American blood should be shed 6,000 miles overseas on a continent that is destined to be ruled by Orientals for Orientals. If the Filipinos are on our conscience, we could lend them money to help create a native defense force, including coastal batteries, submarines, planes and anti-aircraft guns, that would be strong enough to make the Japanese think twice before attempting a conquest. And we could admit all Filipino products into the U. S. duty free in order to provide the islands with foreign exchange to service and liquidate defense loans. We might also persuade the Filipinos to lease naval bases to the British and French, who have a much greater stake in that part of the world than we have. Surely the British, who own Hongkong and Singapore base, and the French, who rule in Indo-China, would not lightly regard a possible Japanese invasion of the Philippines. I will admit this particular proposal is a bit disingenuous, for British and French rule in the Orient will hardly outlast this century. But since the issue is one of power-politics, disingenuousness is not wholly out of place. If Britain and France want to fight a war in the Orient, that is their affair. All I am concerned with is keeping the U. S. from wasting blood and substance over lands not covered by the Monroe Doctrine.

The U. S. as a whole has expressed a disinclination to fight in Europe or Asia: poll after poll has shown that most of our people are willing to settle for "hemisphere" defense and the Monroe Doctrine. There are, however, patriots who think in terms of a "preventive" war; they argue that France and Britain are our first lines of defense, and consider a fight in "the other fellow's backyard" more sensible than a fight in our own. Superficially, this way of looking at things makes sense.

But the case for a preventive war does not survive a calm analysis of all the factors involved. It may be that the U. S. admirals count on the British fleet in the Atlantic to give them a free hand in the far Pacific. And it might indeed prove an annoyance to have the British fleet fall into the hands of a Pan-European dictator. As we have seen, however, the motives for a European or Asiatic or a European *and* Asiatic invasion of North America are practically non-existent. Visions of a Red or a Black Napoleon overrunning the globe belong to the mythology of the anti-Christ, who has yet to make his appearance in human form. The motives for causing trouble in Latin America are more substantial; but we have first to assume the British would hand over their fleet to a conqueror when there is nothing to prevent a quick transference of the whole floating shebang to the free dominions of Canada and Australia. Inasmuch as it is extremely unlikely that a continental European nation will ever get control of the British fleet, we might well defer worrying about such an event until it has happened. We may be sure that the British will abandon their navy only after months of decimation; if and when the dreaded event occurs the Pan-European conqueror will be taking over

a shambles. We could on that distant date begin building ship for ship with our rivals—and still keep close
enough to them to make a sea war in western waters
altogether too risky a thing for them to attempt.

In any case, our frontier is on the sea, not in the mud
or concrete battlements of France. A land war 3,000
miles from home is a terrific consumer of men, material
and money; a sea war, which is necessarily settled by
one or two decisive engagements if it is ever settled at
all, is a cheap—and therefore a democratic—war.
According to the National Economy League, participation in the World War cost the United States a direct
total of $24,135,000,000—or some $42,000,000 a day.
The total cost of the war, including the $13,232,369,-
000 principal and interest of the Allies' unpaid debts,
the pensions and bonuses to veterans, and so on, has
been $55,000,000,000—or more than the current na-
tional debt. A battleship costs $80,000,000, which is a
lot of money. But it would be cheap at the price to
increase our navy to a point of invulnerability. I do not
urge this, for I can't see that any combination of European or Asiatic nations would lightly forget smoldering
animosities at home to engage in a dubious cross-ocean
war in the west. Better to spend smaller amounts of
money on coast defenses, submarines, destroyers, mine-
layers, Caribbean and Aleutian air bases, and long
range bombing planes. Better to lend money to South
America for purposes of building *fuehrer*-proof democratic economies below the equator. Still, if worst comes

to worst, even a two-ocean navy would be cheaper than another overseas crusade of 1917-18 dimensions. As Major George Fielding Eliot has pointed out, even the biggest navy doesn't require millions of men and billions of dollars for ammunition. A navy does not lay down costly daily barrages that thunder for hours, nor does it engage in "wars of position" that require battle lines which stretch over hundreds of miles of the earth's surface. Naval warfare is maneuver warfare: it is, therefore, fought by small, compact units which attempt to choose their ground as Saxe, an army man, chose his ground at Fontenoy, forcing the enemy to come to him on disadvantageous terms. Most important of all, a navy keeps itself out of sight and hearing of the home folks, who are thus not left exposed to the anti-democratic virus of militarism. An army strutting about in uniform has done much to make the Germans a nation of kowtowers and autocrats; but Britain, which has been defended by the out-of-sight-out-of-mind Jackie Tar, has remained as democratic as a caste system society can ever remain.

Air and naval strategy and armament would seem to be less complicated than the subject of army mechanization: anyone can see with Major Eliot that short-range bombers would be less useful to us in repelling attacks from overseas than long-range bombers. And even the tyro can grasp the advantages of owning the Panama Canal. Since we have the canal, our navy need only be superior to the Japanese fleet in the Pacific *or* the combined enemy fleets in the Atlantic; it does not have to be more powerful than the combined tonnage of *all* enemy fleets for the simple reason that it could first cope with its Atlantic enemy, then steam through the canal to deal with the Pacific enemy, or vice versa. Such strategy, the strategy of working the so-called "interior lines," calls for a Canal Zone that is relatively invulnerable, and an air force, a coast defense and a flotilla of submarines and torpedo boats capable of defending one shore while the main battlefleet is attacking the enemy off the other. We don't need to worry about an Atlantic enemy making a junction via Suez with a Pacific enemy, for the moment the Atlantic enemy had steamed into the Red Sea the U. S. fleet could raid the European coast. Nor does a free England figure as a possible Atlantic enemy: Canada is too vulnerable a hostage to permit an Anglo-U. S. war. If some Americans still want a huge two-ocean navy, let them meditate on the implications of that desire. A two-ocean fleet would inevitably be considered a double-size one-ocean fleet by any European or Asiatic power, for it could be assembled quickly as a unit in either ocean. To counter such an aggregation of power, both Japan and our hypothetical European naval enemy would have to double their own fleets as a condition of power-politics survival. The upshot would be a financially debilitating naval race that would certainly bankrupt Europe and Asia and lead to increased world unrest—and in the end we would be no better off from a comparative standpoint.

Latent in all this discussion is the assumption that morality begins at home. Is the assumption Pharisaic? Is it smug? "Internationalists" will say so. Dorothy Thompson, for example, argues that the war in Europe is a moral war between two ideas, two concepts. The first concept is that of a world-wide system of free intercourse, of free or reciprocal trade. The second concept is that of large-scale autarchic units, with weaker nations—Poland, Turkey, Venezuela, and so on—taken as slave dependencies into the "lebensraum," or living space, of master monopolistic nations. Miss Thompson's unspoken assumption is that the U. S. ought, as a Christian nation, to side actively with the states that believe in the first concept.

If there were a breath of realism in Miss Thompson's description of the world, I would agree with her. But observe the lurking hypocrisy in the pretensions that England and France have ever, as nations, been interested in a free intercourse world for everybody. As long as Britain was an outstanding creditor nation, with funds to invest overseas and goods to sell everywhere, she was for the Open Door, for Manchesterism and all the rest. But when the shoe pinched, as it did after the World War, England junked the gold standard, devalued her currency to a point that provoked counter-devaluations in Japan and the U. S., and turned to "Empire Free Trade," which was the Ottawa version of "lebensraum," the autarchy of a rich empire. Czechoslovakia, long celebrated as the lone "outpost of democracy" in central Europe, was one of the first European states to experiment with agricultural autarchy—and the experiment worked real hardship in Hungary and other Danubian countries. As for the French, they have always regarded their African and Asiatic empires as part of a Gallic "lebensraum"; the French saddled the supposedly "free intercourse" world with the quota system long before Hjalmar Horace Greeley Schacht showed what really could be done with the quota idea. Meanwhile the British and Dutch rubber and tin producers, banded together in cartels, took their monopolistic toll of world trade whenever it was possible to keep their own "chiselers" in line. If all this constituted a "trend toward world organization on the basis of equality," as Miss Thompson supposes, then I'm the left-handed member of the Siamese twins. True, the U. S., with its Grundy tariff, did nothing to make the world safe for international competition; we have no right to point the finger of scorn at Britain and France. But the point to be made here is that the West did its collective best to squeeze Germany into its autarchic madness: Schacht's measures were a hopeless debtor's adaptation of the tricks used by everyone. It is one thing to say the world "ought" to free its merchants from nationalistic shackles. But trade is normally done by a circulating medium, and a country without gold to back its circulating medium must resort to restrictive dodges to protect the home-value of its money. Nations can only afford free trade as long as they are selling approximately as much as they are buying; else they will discover queer things happening to their price levels, the value of their securities, and so on. I will believe in the reality of Miss Thompson's analysis when I see the U. S. disgorging its gold, or when I observe Britain permitting the Japanese to market any and all goods in India and Australia without squeals from Manchester, or when the French throw open their own quota-protected "lebensraum" to all comers, including the U. S. wheat farmer who can out-compete the French peasant by such a wide margin that Dakota would immediately capture the Paris bakery trade hands down.

Knowing what the World War did to the free trade ideal, I venture to predict that more tariffs, more quotas, more competitive currency devaluations, more repudiations of international loans (if any are floated), more autarchy, more bilateral barter, will come out of the present war regardless of who wins. I am hoping for the opposite, but meanwhile the best the U. S. can do is to try to preserve a relatively large reciprocal trade area in the western hemisphere. If Europe ever shows signs of coming to her senses, it would be a relatively easy thing for us to lend gold to support her currencies and to enable her to reorganize on a free intercourse basis. We do not need to fight and demoralize our own economy in order to put our weight behind sound moves toward a Manchesterian world.

Everyone is now talking of a United States of Europe—a real "union" with one police power, one system of courts, one currency system, one tax area, and one sovereignty. The United States of America should welcome such a union, for it would make possible some settled and mutually profitable customs and currency agreements between two sides of the Atlantic Ocean. A United States of Europe might even presage a wider union of the whole Atlantic world. But the U. S. should beware underwriting any peace in Europe that merely involves a reshuffling of old boundaries or another punitive crippling of defeated powers. And any attempt to revive the old League of Nations, as distinct from a *union of states*, should be regarded as a poison-baited trap from the outset. For a League (witness our own Articles of Confederation) solves no problems; it merely provides a new and more centralized arena for old-fashioned balance-of-power deals under the table. A Bismarck and a Metternich would discover themselves quite at home in a League of Nations; for the whispered word, the secret understanding, the fingered pulse, can come out of cloakrooms as well as chancelleries. Jockeying for balance-of-power position must always go on in a League, for when individual state sovereignties aren't surrendered to one supra-authority the struggle to establish individual bargaining power continues to have free play. This struggle generates the heats and frictions of de facto alliances and counter-alliances, all backed by the latent threat of force. And the minute a real issue divides the powers, then good-by to the League.

I will be charged, naturally, with having taken a "let Europe stew in her own juice" attitude in this chapter. But again it must be said that proximity breeds primary responsibility. Besides, Europe does not want permanent interference by the U. S.; in 1919 Lloyd George and Clemenceau wished to God that Woodrow Wilson would shut up and go home. Personally, I can understand their point of view: I love the Bill of Rights, but I should hate to see it interpreted and enforced here by a Polish-Hungarian-German-Yugoslav balance-of-power bloc exercising de facto control in a world government. In any event, U. S. interference in European affairs merely results in underwriting one European cook as against another. Our participation in the World War merely tossed our men and money into a stew that grew more and more offensive the longer it simmered. If we had gone into the League of Nations, we might have made the attempt to persuade France and England to behave more leniently toward Weimar Germany. But sooner or later the question of the interallied war debts would have divided us: Uncle Shylock would have been Uncle Shylock no matter where his representatives parked their hats. And, seizing on the division among the World War victors, the

"have-nots" would surely have gone their own buccaneering way.

Judging from the record, no American is in a position to refuse to "let Europe stew in its own juice";
Europe will do its own cooking regardless of American
attitude. As General Hugh S. Johnson has said, the
great strategic highway of the Danube, the passes of
the Alps, the flank routes through the lowlands of Bel-
gium and Holland, the barrier of the Pyrenees, the
basin of the Mediterranean, the stronghold of Verdun
and the terrain of the Black Forest are all squares on
an immemorial checkerboard. To this list of squares
the General might have added the Dardanelles-Bos-
porus water route between Rumania, Russia and the
Mediterranean. With or without our interference, the
great checker game will go on until Europe can be
unified by force of arms or force of despair from
within. When that unification comes we should not be
niggardly in welcoming it. We should stand ready to
extend our economic aid on one condition: that trade
barriers be lowered everywhere.

But how are we to keep out of war if our emotions
are outraged by bombing attacks on civilians, or if fears
of an Allied defeat begin to tear at our hearts and
nerves? Personally, I put little trust in "neutrality"
legislation, although I am glad for the cash-and-carry
law we already have. There are, of course, loopholes
in this law: there is nothing, for example, to keep U. S.

citizens from lending money to, say, Andorra, for the purchase of war materials destined ultimately for the Allies. Still, the law is better than nothing. And there is cause for hope in a more cynical consideration of power-politics reality. I refer to the U. S. position as *pro tem* watchdog for "white" interests in the Far East. As long as Japan is busy shrewdly estimating the degree of the confusion of Europe, a State Department committed to the Open Door and the defense of the Philippines will hardly range itself with those who want to send a military expedition to Europe. Balance-of-power thus tends to preserve our isolation from Europe's troubles where more idealistic—or should I say reasonable?—considerations fail. Moreover, many of our business men—Weir, Rockefeller—have had their bellyful of war: they know that net profits fall away the minute war taxes are put into effect; they know, too, that plant capacity which is enlarged for military purposes results only in severe post-war financial headache.

There remains the possibility that, given a Fascist victory in Europe, the idea of the thing would gather such momentum that American democracy would be overwhelmed from within. Fascist technique is disintegrative technique: it works by revolutionary means within a nation. So far, however, the disintegrative technique has only served as a weapon inside weak contiguous nations whose only alternatives are catastrophic punishment in war or capitulation to revolutionaries. The disintegrative technique broke Austria and Spain (much as the U. S. frown has broken regimes in the Caribbean region), but it has only served to solidify anti-Fascist opinion in France and Britain. Faced with a Fascist Europe, America would certainly not meekly surrender its government to a Fritz Kuhn or a Father Coughlin. The government might be forced to institute foreign trade controls and military policies leading to further centralization of power. But war would centralize power in this country far more quickly than the threat of a Fascist Europe. If Americans despair of their democracy so easily that they contemplate its extinction merely because an anti-democratic idea is abroad in Europe and Asia, then the democracy is doomed anyway.

Half Steel, Half Putty

IF I am against involvement of the United States in Europe's quarrels, it is not out of any sense that we can afford to sit back and preen ourselves forever on the good fortune of being flanked by "two broad oceans." We may live at a distance from the cramped and rigid economies of the Old World, but we most emphatically need a limber, responsive price-system at home if a maximum of goods and services are to be exchanged for a minimum of John Doe's money. It would admittedly be better if the limber unit could be world-wide in scope; but for reasons which are either explicit or inherent in the preceding chapter I have no hope of living to see the creation of a world free-trade area. I assume that we must make the best of what we have, which brings me to the question of monopoly and the U. S. continental economic domain.

For five years the New Deal, bemused by the Chamber-of-Commerce neo-fascism of NRA, seemed bent on dodging the issue of monopoly. Then, at the tag end of 1937, it suddenly found its line—a line that was to result in the TNEC, or Temporary National Economic Committee. Because of the alarums and excursions of a war-wary chief executive and State De-

partment, the positive accomplishments of this committee have gone practically unnoticed. Nevertheless, the
fact that the TNEC has been dipping an assiduous nose
into U. S. business practices has already resulted in a
great deal of unpublicized good. Mr. Leon Henderson,
the SEC commissioner who has been the guiding light
of the TNEC, has no particular power. But Mr. Henderson has stuck grimly to one idea—that of conveying
to big business executives the notion that quasi-
monopolies can price themselves out of potentially
profitable markets by adhering to the conventional
policy of charging all the traffic will bear. Mr. Henderson's pertinacity has borne fruit: U. S. Steel, bellwether
of the entire U. S. economic system, has twice foregone
the temptation of leading the steel industry in a general
price rise.

Two years ago only a Pollyanna would have believed that Mr. Henderson had a chance of bringing
Big Steel to his side. True, the administration had
commenced to go after "monopoly" with a sudden
fearful war whoop. But when Robert H. Jackson, then
chief trust-buster for the Department of Justice, made
his first vociferous speeches on the subject of monopoly,
the Big Business community answered by insinuating
that the whole anti-monopoly crusade was part of a
monstrous shell game. The shells, so the imputation
ran, were three in number—their names were "anti-
monopoly," "voluntary co-operation between business
and government," and "collectivism," or New Deal

socialism. The pea of ultimate Administration policy was presumably under one of the shells, but no one could quite tell which. Moreover, it was commonly believed there was a magician in the room—a Houdini —masked as Franklin Delano Roosevelt. This magician, so the canard ran, was quite capable of sneaking the pea away altogether.

But the New Deal was not engaged in a shell game; it was merely seeking to square its desire—the highly laudable desire of more opportunity and more riches for everybody—with the realities of a modern economic system that was part monopolistic and part competitive, "half steel, half putty." In searching for its line the New Deal moved blindly and confusedly. Speeches and gestures often canceled one another. On one day the President would denounce the holding company; the next day he would advocate round-table conferences with business men to "plan" production. Some Democrats in high place were for the Guffey Act, which was designed to result in price stabilization for the ailing soft coal operators. Other Democrats caviled at U. S. Steel's "price umbrella," under which the rest of the steel industry huddled to keep out of the competitive wet. The terrible baiter of economic royalists, Mr. Ickes, advocated oil conservation; federal prosecutors in Wisconsin, however, jumped on sixteen oil companies for alleged price fixing. The confusion of the Administration was reflected in the attitudes of its enemies: in the pages of the New York *Herald*

Tribune Walter Lippmann hoped that Robert Jackson's "interesting" speeches indicated a return to good Jeffersonian or Brandeisean economic doctrine, while Dorothy Thompson, thinking in the misleading terms of European analogy, promptly accused poor Mr. Jackson of copying the demagogy of Paul Joseph Goebbels.

The easiest way to explain the anti-monopoly campaign of early 1938 was to mutter: "Politics." And, indeed, the alacrity with which Mr. Roosevelt seized on the old Bryanite and Populist slogans did look suspicious. Business men at the end of 1937 had started to grumble about a "Roosevelt depression." Dirty words were passed at the December meetings of the National Association of Manufacturers in New York, and there were mutterings in the Duquesne Club at Pittsburgh. The Administration quite naturally needed a backfire—and, since NRA had flopped, the anti-monopoly campaign seemed made to its hand. But the quick-starters who dismissed the anti-monopoly crusade as just a political move, part of the eternal dumb show of the grand old game of using your influence to beat down the other fellow's influence, were mistaken. Actually, the New Dealers—specifically, the Jackson-Corcoran-Cohen-Henderson "well-integrated" group —meant business. They had decided the time had come to strike a blow for freedom, lest the country be turned over to fascist or communist collectivists. As we shall see, they were seeking to make the competitive system really competitive.

The main reason why there was so much confusion in the public mind about the moves in Washington was the portmanteau, catch-all quality of "monopoly" as a word. Rolled over on the tongues of a hundred political orators, Mon-op-o-lee has always seemed to mask an accusation that all business indulges in monopolistic practices. In early 1938 there were three main groups in Washington fighting to gain acceptance for three different views of monopoly. The Federal Trade Commission, which believed in enforcing the anti-trust laws, fought for one theory of a complex phenomenon. The Donald Richberg group, which had nostalgic hankerings for the NRA, fought for another; this group believed that de facto cartelization of industry was here to stay and that government ought to sit in as a supervisor of hours, wages, prices, what-not. Leon Henderson's group, however, believed in an "as if" approach to the subject. Granted that huge industrial aggregations with the power to control prices (and therefore to limit or expand production) were here to stay, it might be possible to persuade or compel these aggregations to "administer" their prices at a point calculated to result in big sales at low unit profit. They might be persuaded to act "as if" they were competitors. Most people tend to think in terms of polar antitheses, such as "planning" versus "laissez faire." But Mr. Henderson conceived the fight in the New Deal to be a fight between "planning for slavery" and "planning for freedom." NRA had planned for slavery; but a "planned-free" system was something else again. In the old days the Federal government had "planned" the donation of sections of the public domain to worthy individuals in order to give a dynamic impulse to capitalist expansion. The draining off of excess labor into the American West had incidentally served to put a cushion under wages—which amounted to governmental "interference" with the market. After 1910 the "planning" by states and counties of a great network of roads had effectively subsidized an automobile industry. Presumably there were still "planning" dodges of this sort available to a government trying to get the U. S. business machine off dead center.

Mr. Henderson was, of course, trying to penetrate a fog. For his picture of the U. S. business system, which is a picture with a one-to-one correspondence to reality, was not the picture that existed in the heads of the American business men. Taken as a whole, the business men of the U. S. think they are living in a competitive world. They have never stopped to square what they learned long ago with the practices that are under their noses—and under their guiding hands. They believe sincerely in competition. But the competition they believe in is not ordinary price competition; it is quality, or brand-name, competition for dominance

Half Steel, Half Putty

in the market at a relatively stable price. A man selling Lucky Strikes or Kelvinator refrigerators or Pontiacs may charge the same prices for comparable brands or models as the store or agency on the opposite corner. Yet the two stores or agencies are certainly "competing" for the available customers, which is competition enough for the average business man. If he is desperate or daring this business man may shade the price of his competitor by any number of tricks: he may, for example, throw in a present, or an extra. And his wholesaler is frequently willing to accommodate him by giving him a cost-saving advantage. Indeed, the art of price shading is a highly developed art; it includes advertising allowances, freight allowances, turn-in allowances, discounts on volume, reciprocal buying agreements ("You scratch my back and I'll scratch yours"), cash discounts, extended credit, direct rebates, gifts of trading stamps, offering a baker's dozen, sharing promotion costs, and so on, ad infinitum. An ingenious iconoclast might with good reason turn Thurman Arnold's "Folklore of Capitalism" quite around and say that we honor monopoly and secretly practice competition. Hidden competition, however, can hardly be as effective an economic governor as the old higgling of the market of pre-Civil War capitalism. And the norms still stand: the business man doesn't want to be caught cutting prices. His brothers regard price competition as chiseling, not as something that is real or valid competition.

The American Stakes

The business man tends to regard the open chiseler as a wretch, a maverick, a destroyer of morale. But he fails to apply the tag "monopolist" to the opposite of the chiseler. His conditioned reflexes warn him that this would be to damn a "good" man with an emotive word that has evil connotations. The old common law frowned on "monopoly" long before the writing of the Sherman Act, and the business man cannot easily cut himself off from the stream of history.

All of this is quite understandable when we recall what most college-trained business men learned as sophomores in Econ. 1. Let us picture the standard Econ. 1 course as it was ten, fifteen or twenty years ago. Let us recall ourselves as students with pencils poised but minds asleep as the professor droned on about a world of "perfect" competition, in which buyers inevitably got the benefit of spirited bidding for their coy dollars. This world of perfect competition was explained by a few honored classical concepts—the law of supply and demand, the law of diminishing returns, the theory of marginal utility. These concepts reinforced a central axiom: that Competition is the Life of Trade.

Along about the fifth month the professor got around to the subject of monopoly. Monopoly was a villain—an ugly creature who had ruled the roost in the days of mercantilism but who had happily been banished in England with the coming of the industrial revolution. The villain persisted on the European continent in the form of cartels, but that was because Europeans—and especially the Germans, who had learned a trick or two from our own Alexander Hamilton—were benighted economic heathen who had never read Cobden and Bright on the virtues of free trade. Sometimes the villain managed to rear his ugly head in the U. S., where the protectionist philosophy was unfortunately respected. The villain was pictured as a conniver who tricked his fellow citizens to corner the sources of supply of a given commodity. Once a corner had been effected, the villain jacked up prices beyond all conscience. But the American public was pure at heart, and could be counted on to get wise to the cornerer. Economic sin in the U. S. usually provoked a successful crusade, with the villain pried loose from his spoils. Witness, said the professor, the restoration of competition in a field that had once been monopolized by the elder Rockefeller's Standard Oil Company.

Confusion about monopoly is even more understandable when it exists among the so-called practical, or self-made, men who have never studied economics in the schools. The average man of fifty or fifty-five may never think about monopoly unless someone yells the word at him. But when he does think of it he has in mind a stereotype created by half a century of political oratory and journalistic muckraking. He has, perhaps, listened to William Jennings Bryan or the elder La Follette as a young man. Or, if not, he has certainly read a speech or two on the subject by William E.

Borah. What the average man of fifty has in mind when you mention monopoly to him is the sort of thing that Henry Demarest Lloyd inveighed against in "Wealth Against Commonwealth" in 1894—the classical aggressive monopoly of Standard Oil, which had put its competitors out of business by all sorts of snide practices, including the taking of rebates from the railroads that carried its products in bulk. The average man of fifty has in mind the railroads as they figured in the literature of the western Populists and early Progressives—the Southern Pacific, for example, when the young Hiram Johnson was blasting it as the Octopus. He has in mind the "trusts" that Theodore Roosevelt went out to "bust" with the Big Stick. He has in mind a group of girthy plug-uglies, drawn by the young Mr. Hearst's cartoonist F. Opper and known as the "interests." These plug-uglies conspired over groaning festive boards to effect "combinations in restraint of trade." The Sherman Anti-trust Law of 1890 and the Clayton Act of 1914 were supposed to have outlawed conspiracies in restraint of trade and other "unfair" practices. And the Federal Trade Commission had been created to serve as a watchdog. But meanwhile there were big combinations—such as Judge Gary's U. S. Steel Corporation and, later, General Motors—that were, somehow, "good" trusts. These did not "unreasonably" restrain trade. They did not aggressively try to put all competitors out of business; in fact, they were glad to share the field in order to create good will for themselves. Both Theodore Roosevelt and Chief Justice White of the Supreme Court had made an exception of the "good" trust that did not seriously impair competition. And with this distinction in mind the average man dismisses the "bigness" of the corporate units that took shape in the first quarter of this century. They do not "seriously" impair competition.

Traditionally, there have been three kinds of monopoly. There is the "natural" monopoly that depends on sewing up title to certain bottleneck portions of the earth's surface. This might be called the geographical type of monopoly. There is the source-of-supply monopoly, which in most cases might be called geological. Most classic "corners" have been based on source-of-supply monopoly. And third, there is the old-fashioned proprietary monopoly.

Railroads and public utilities are the conspicuous examples of "natural," or geographical, monopoly. A railroad from Crackerville to Lyons Corners owns its right-of-way; no one else can send trains over this particular right-of-way without the railroad's permission. An electric light and power company usually controls the entire sale of kilowatt-hours within its particular area. And a telephone company normally has all the telephone business in a given town or city.

The geological monopoly is one that controls the full effective supply of a raw material within the earth:

The American Stakes

International Nickel is a quasi-monopoly of the geological type, as is the Climax Molybdenum Company, which owns practically all the good molybdenum in the U. S. Insofar as it controls the paying bauxite deposits on the North American continent, the Aluminum Company of America is a geological monopoly.

Finally, the proprietary monopoly is one that controls its products, or its sales territories, through rights of patent or rights of grant. When General Electric owned all the good tungsten-bulb patents it controlled an electric-lamp monopoly. The Massachusetts Bay Company, which had a charter from the King of England to exploit a strip of America stretching from ocean to ocean, was a proprietary monopoly through its possession of an exclusive grant.

Most of the federal machinery for handling monopoly cases has grown out of the traditional monopoly thinking. Regulatory commissions such as the ICC have been set up to restrain the "natural," or geographical, type of monopoly. The proprietary monopoly has not had much attention, owing primarily to a widespread feeling that the inventor who applies for a patent has a pretty good right to whatever he can get for the product of his brains. As for the source-of-supply monopoly, the Federal Trade Commission was set up to prevent powerful companies from getting a stranglehold on specific commodities or services through "unfair" competitive tricks. Laws were once thought sufficient to prevent or restrain the development of source-of-supply monopolies. The Sherman Anti-trust Law of 1890 and the Federal Trade Commission and Clayton acts of 1914 are eloquent testimony to the hold that the legalistic and moralistic approach to monopoly has had on the people.

But when the members of the "well-integrated group" among inner circle New Dealers speak of monopoly they are not thinking primarily about geographical, geological, or proprietary monopolies, nor are they thinking in legalistic or moralistic terms. When SEC commissioner Leon Henderson, and Robert Jackson, and Gardiner Means of the National Resources Committee talk about monopolistic practices they are not thinking of the classical "cornerer" who "sits upon the sources of supply" and puts a single-barreled high-priced gun to the head of society. They are not thinking in terms of the old-time professorial discussion at all, for that discussion neatly and falsely counterpoises the polar abstractions of "perfect" competition and "perfect" monopoly, neither of which very often exists in nature.

The truth of the matter is that Henderson and others of the so-called "radical" wing of the New Deal have become aware of the vast middle ground of "imperfect" competition for which the newest economists are now using the peculiar terms of "duopoly"—or "two to sell"—and "oligopoly"—or "few to sell." They know, as the old-time professor did not, that a world of "administered prices," of basing-point systems, of "follow the leader" pricing tactics, of reciprocal buying ("you scratch my back by buying my steel rails and I'll scratch your back by shipping on your railroad"), is not the world postulated in the books of the classical theorists. And they also know why the "little fellow" must be careful to follow the "open prices" that the Big Two or the Big Three post with the trade association. They know that if the little fellow doesn't follow the Big Two or the Big Three he may be "competed" out of existence by the companies with the superior resources.

From all this the radical New Dealer assumes that perfect competition, far from being the rule on the industrial side of our economy, is now the exception to the rule. But the radical New Dealer still uses the word "monopoly"—"one to sell"—when he is talking about "oligopoly," or "few to sell." The reason is obvious: if you made a speech denouncing oligopoly no one would know what you were talking about.

What the radical New Dealers are complaining about is not monopoly as such. They are complaining about price rigidity. And it is true that an inductive study of price trends bears out Henry Wallace's contention— that the price structure in the U. S. economy is "half of steel and half of putty." Stiff, rigid, stable prices are as much a commonplace to steelmen, to cement manufacturers, to sellers of nickel and sulphur, as fluctuating prices are to the farmer. And the business man who fervently denies that he is a monopolist will, in the next breath, boast that his particular business is a "clean" business—meaning that the "price chiselers" have been driven out of the field.

Since the radical New Deal critique hinges on pricing policy, not on corporate bigness as such, it naturally makes actual market behavior, not hypothetical moral intent, the field of its investigations and the source of its recommendations. An industry may be obeying all the anti-trust and anti-monopoly laws on the books, but if its pricing policy is out of line with the pricing policy in other industries the radical New Dealer feels that he must do something about it. If prices are rapidly rising in one section of the economy and precipitously falling in another, the relationships of inter-group buying power are seriously disturbed. And everybody winds up by consuming less. The problem is to demonstrate this to people who think in terms of angels and devils, or bigness and littleness. As a beginning, the radical New Dealer would have the government push its TNEC inquiry into the present status of competition and the comparative behavior of prices to an exhaustive conclusion. As Robert Jackson put it in 1937, you need a Pecora investigation before you can prove to the voters the need for an SEC. Pending action by Congress or wide self-discipline by "price leaders" in the trade associations, the radical New Dealers will go on amassing their own data about pricing policy in the U. S. economy. And from this data certain broad trends will probably continue to emerge.

To establish the main points of reference on the trend

map, let us follow the radical New Dealer as he investigates the 1929-33 price and production records of two industries—cement and cotton textiles. A comparison of these two industries will give dramatic point to the difference between an industry that can control its pricing and an industry that cannot. With the stock-market break in 1929, wholesale prices on cotton goods started falling immediately. And as wholesale prices fell, production slacked off as certain marginal firms were wiped out. But the point to be noted in this connection is that production did not fall proportionately with prices. In 1932 prices were at 54 per cent of the 1926 level, while production was at 75 per cent of its 1926 level.* Net profits for the industry as a whole had been $76,000,000 in 1927; in 1930 there were net *losses* of $92,000,000.

The reason why cotton textiles is such a shifty, chancy business is something known to the trade as "volume mania." Even in the year 1932, when the depression reached rock bottom and customers were everywhere in hiding, the industry operated at 80 per cent of capacity. Why? Because each operator, knowing that in a freely fluctuating market he is powerless to effect the price for cotton textiles by any single decision of his own, invariably tries to produce and sell just as much as he can without running up his operating costs. Quite naturally he calculates his expected profit or loss in re-

* Production indexes for cotton textiles are based on raw-cotton consumption figures.

lation to the going or expected market price, and the only way he can raise his profits or cut his losses is by keeping up production as long as the market price will more than cover his operating costs. After all, *if he doesn't produce the goods someone else will.* But the result of some 800 corporations and some 1,000 mills with 27,000,000 spindles all pursuing the same policy is drastic overproduction, a lowering of both the going and the expected price—and losses all around.

As someone has put it, "the boys can't seem to get together." No one producer can afford to limit production as long as other producers are maintaining or even increasing production. No one producer can hold or increase his prices when his competitors are lowering their prices. The Cotton Textile Institute, which was organized in 1926, proved powerless to whip chiselers into line. And since no single producer controls more than 3 per cent of the industry, no one is in a position to effect "price leadership." The NRA did enforce some stability, but the Supreme Court removed the props. As for the cotton-goods merchandisers, they are no help at all. For the merchandisers get a commission on total sales, not on mill profits, and in time of falling demand their way of keeping up the commission-paying volume is to shade the price. Thus they aid and abet the volume mania of the producers. It's hell for the manufacturer, and hard on labor, but the result of the anarchy is cheap goods, which is nice for the ultimate consumer. It is also presumably more healthy for the economy as a whole for a few companies to go bankrupt than for all the companies to keep in business by holding up the consumer. When price competition rules the market, the benefits from industrial efficiency are passed on to the consumer in the form of price cuts, instead of flowing preponderantly into the tills of big ownership. Price competition thus diffuses the savings from technological advance over a wider population area and tends to keep wealthy individuals from saving more than they can profitably invest.

Now let us look at cement, which is at the other extreme of the market. The cement industry first felt the economic pinch in the summer of 1930, and output for the year 1931 dropped to 76 per cent of the 1926 level. Prices, however, were slow to follow. Eventually they, too, commenced to sag, reaching 77 in 1932—the low year for the industry. Meanwhile production had dropped precipitously to 47.

With the coming of the New Deal the cement men began to adjust their prices upward, carrying them to 86 per cent of the 1926 level for the year 1933. This upward movement was not in response to increased demand, for though prices rose production kept going down. When prices reached 86, output had fallen to the low point of 39. The cement industry operated at 76 per cent of capacity during 1926, at 28 per cent in 1932, and at 29 per cent in 1935. Meanwhile the comparable cotton-textile figures were 95 per cent for 1926, 80 for 1932, and 91 for 1935. Obviously, the cement industry is not cursed with the volume mania of the cotton-textile industry.

Stability is achieved in the cement industry by use of the multiple basing-point system. Sixty-odd places in the country are used as basing points. Mills in a basing-point territory charge the customer the base price, plus the freight from the basing point to the customer's door. Thus delivered prices in a given basing-point territory remain the same, no matter whether the mill is between the basing point and the customer or on the other side of the basing point. If the mill is closer to the customer than the basing point itself, the saving on the freight charge will go into the manufacturer's profit. Through this system it is impossible for the customer to get the natural advantage of having a mill closer to him than he is to the basing point.

When a cement mill wants to sell outside of its own territory, it computes its quotations from the base price of the mill that controls in the territory where the sale is being made and absorbs the difference in the freight rate. Freight rate books are issued by the Cement Institute to show approximate freight charges to all places within reasonable distances from basing points. As a result of the multiple basing-point system, the delivered price of cement is the same no matter from whom you buy.

Just as a plethora of manufacturers and an absence of big units make the cotton-textile industry fiercely competitive, so a limited number of manufacturers and the presence of a Big Five makes the cement industry an easy one to keep in line. Cement's Big Five operated fifty-nine of the industry's 175 plants in 1929 and controlled 40 per cent of the total capacity. No one of the remaining seventy-two companies controlled more than 3.5 per cent of capacity. The inference is clear: a competitor with 3.5 per cent of capacity would step warily before engaging in a price war with rivals capable of producing 40 per cent. It is reasonable to suppose that cement prices have remained steady not because of collusion but because the little fellows in the industry know what is good for their economic health.

The cement industry and the cotton-textile industry may stand as typical of the two incompatible trends that are pulling the price system apart. Where price rigidity exists—as it does in iron and steel, agricultural machinery, and brick and tiles—there is normally a huge drop in production when the business cycle turns down. The corollaries of this decrease in production are a marked decrease in total payrolls and few bankruptcies. Where price flexibility rules the market—as it does in foods, leather, and textiles of all sorts—there is no staggering drop in production during depression. And the corollaries of sustained production are a relative steadiness in total payrolls plus more numerous bankruptcies.

Whether to brave the decrease in production or the increase in bankruptcies is a choice that politicians have a hard time making. But the practical advantages of remaining solvent must seem paramount to most business men. Hence the desire and the drive for stable prices. This drive manifests itself in many forms. Rigidity in wholesale prices compels rigidity in the retail field as a natural defensive reflex: when your source of supply maintains his prices you feel you have a moral right to maintain yours. Hence, if you are a retailer and your competitor across the street is cutting prices on brand-name products, you will welcome a Miller-Tydings law to force "retail price maintenance." If you run a Chevrolet agency and are compelled to offer a good fat turn-in allowance in order to sell a new car, you don't want to see the used-car market demoralized by dumping. If you run a small bookshop, you are furious when department stores sell $2.50 novels at a "loss leader" price of $1.98. With price cutting threatening your solvency, you might very well feel like conspiring with your competitors to maintain steady prices.

Probably very few outright conspiracies to fix prices actually exist in either the retail or the wholesale field. It remains a fact, however, that in wholesale industries whose price structures are stable you will usually discover a Big Three or a Big Five, or even a Big One. In nickel and nickel alloys the International Nickel Company controls around 70 per cent of output; the price of nickel ingots hasn't changed since 1929. Two companies —Texas Gulf Sulphur and Freeport Sulphur—control about 90 per cent of sulphur production; the price of sulphur did not change from 1926 to 1938. Steel companies have observed the multiple basing-point practices of U. S. Steel, not by collusive agreements at "Gary dinners," but simply because they know that any retaliatory price shading by the stronger companies might end up in disaster for the weaker companies. In farm equipment there is a Big Four—International Harvester, Deere & Company, Minneapolis-Moline Power Implement, and J. I. Case. These four have not permitted farm-equipment prices to move up and down in relation to the price of cotton or the price of wheat. Allis-Chalmers, however, has been giving them a little real competition in recent months.

Back in the days of Adam Smith it was assumed that profits were the reward for taking risk. But with the "institutionalizing" of capitalism there has developed what one economist has called a "revulsion against risk." Producers not only want but think they have a right to expect a price that will cover (1) direct operating costs for labor and raw materials; (2) overhead out-of-pocket costs such as taxation, insurance, and interest charges; (3) depreciation and maintenance overhead; and (4) a "reasonable" profit. A price war naturally hits profits first, then overhead charges. Even if the union won't let you cut wages, price can sink to a point where it just covers operating costs before it will pay you to shut down your plant. Hence in case of extremity an operator will go on producing goods as long as he gets something more than direct operating costs—some margin to help him pay the fixed charges that he has to pay whether he is producing or not.

The moralistic concomitant of the "revulsion against risk" is the feeling that price wars are evil and price chiselers immoral. There is good reason for this feeling: price cutting is far more dangerous today than it was in the days of merchant capitalism. In the durable goods industries expensive capital equipment accounts for an ever larger proportion of costs. Hence in these industries you not only have to make your operating expenses in order to cover raw materials and labor but you also have to charge income with large sums for depreciation and pay out a good deal in fixed capital charges. Percentagewise, the overhead costs plus profits for manufacturing industries went up in the decade before 1929, while the percentage accounted for by direct costs went down. Paradoxically, this means that the margin for price chiseling also got larger and more tempting as the overhead and profits grew and the bottom set by the direct operating costs dropped lower.

Under such conditions, where the spread between desired income and absolutely necessary income is large, a price war can rage for a long time before anyone is forced to admit defeat. And while raging, a price war in durable-goods industries can eat up great blocks of capital and finally wreck all but a few favored producers. Moreover, price cutting does not always bring out the expected buyers. Lowered prices are interpreted as signs of weakness, and the potential buyer tends to skip the first cut and wait for the next one to come along and make the goods still cheaper. The potential durable-goods buyer can afford to wait, while the man whose shirts and socks are wearing out cannot. Hence the durable-goods price cutter discovers he is competing against his own future price. Once price cutting starts, the process may become a rout. So the producer decides it is better not to tempt fate. Better reach an understanding to limit the field, keep prices up, and cover your costs in times of recession. In time people will have to buy, and you will get your share of the lump of business then.

All of this may explain why price rigidity tends to be the norm for the durable-goods industries. But plausible or not, the explanation doesn't help the economy. For when some prices fall drastically while others remain sticky, the normal exchange of goods between different groups in the economy is disrupted. Everybody loses. Farmers and producers of raw materials lose in purchasing power because their excessive volume of production destroys unit income. The manufacturer loses in purchasing power because his high prices, while they maintain and increase his real unit income, do not multiply themselves over enough units to increase his wealth. This is not mere theorizing: the physical volume of goods that could be purchased by farmers and raw-material producers, on the one hand, and by manufacturing labor and capital, on the other, dropped one-third or more between 1929 and 1933. Which means that the real purchasing power in "net barter terms of trade" of both groups in 1933 was less than two-thirds what it had been in 1929. Presumably managers and owners still had more income than they could spend on consumers' goods. Theoretically they could have invested their surplus in new capital equipment and so given employment (and purchasing power) to others. But actually capital issues fell to practically nothing by the end of this period. Even in the flush Twenties capital goods had no direct relation to the volume of savings. From 1922 to 1929 savings increased from year to year, yet plant investment did not increase in proportion. The excess money moved overseas to rehabilitate Germany and to pay for Peruvian bonds; or it circulated in Wall Street, bidding up prices of existing stocks. The whole business ended in stalemate until political pressure intervened to alter trends.

If durable-goods prices tend to be so inexorably sticky, why not tackle the problem by pulling the normally wobbly farm prices up to them? That was and is the method of Henry Wallace and the proponents of crop limitation. The method has its rough justice; and early in the Roosevelt regime it seemed to be working. But under the classical theory, true economic health depends, as we have seen, on progressively lowered prices in all sectors of the economy, especially during depressions. Unless wages went continuously up, a universal stabilization of prices on a high plateau would mean progressively higher dividends as technological advance lowered costs. The result would be a continuing concentration of wealth in the hands of the few, since 78 per cent of all corporate dividends went in 1929 to .357 per cent of the population. Balance between spending and investment, so necessary if we are to have both a market for goods and new goods for the market, would thus be destroyed.

If we accept this theory, the conclusion is that the government must whack at sticky prices, anyway, no matter what Mr. Wallace does in the special case of the farmers. Nearly all of the New Dealers are agreed on this. Members of the Federal Trade Commission, however, still stand by the guns of the pre-War Progressive epoch so far as means are concerned; they believe in legislative action to prevent concentration of economic power, not in price whacking simply taken by itself. If you talk with members of the Federal Trade Commission you come out with the idea that bang-up enforcement of the anti-trust laws would do a lot to limber up the capitalist system. These men point to the words of the Sherman law, which supposedly makes monopoly and also *any attempt to monopolize* illegal. They point to the Clayton Act, which aims at outlawing price discrimination. Unfortunately from their point of view, the courts have riddled both the Sherman and Clayton acts. Although Justice Day's minority opinion in the case of U. S. *vs.* U. S. Steel Corporation contends that size per se constitutes violation of the Sherman law, the majority opinion of the Supreme Court implies that size must be accompanied by an overt act, a proved conspiracy to combine in restraint of trade. Section 2 of the Clayton Act outlawed any discriminatory, pricing tactics that would "substantially lessen competition or tend to create a monopoly." But the courts said that you had to prove, first, the existence of widespread failure in an industry before you could get a decision in your favor.

In other words, you had to fill and produce the graveyard in order to prove that competition had been lessened—which offers another case of locking the barn after the horse has disappeared.

Hampered as they are by judicial interpretation and reinterpretation, some members of the Federal Trade Commission want new legislation that will redefine "undue" and "unreasonable" restraint of trade in terms of the percentage of business done by a company in its field. They would like to see bigness made illegal per se; they would like to see the ideas of Justice Brandeis triumph and U. S. industry taken out of the hands of Big Threes or Big Fives and returned to the relatively small, competitive operating unit. They would like to make it legally impossible for any company to become powerful enough to exercise "price leadership."

A considerable number of New Dealers still hold out more or less secretly for the NRA principle, for the so-called "Richberg plan." Accepting concentration of wealth and power as inherent in the facts of modern technology and the mass market, members of this group would suspend or rewrite the anti-trust laws and allow business men to get together to ration production and regulate wages and hours—provided the federal government has the right to regulate the regulators. In one sense the Richberg school would encourage the growth of oligopoly, as the NRA undoubtedly encouraged it. But it believes the federal regulatory power could ensure decent minimum wage and maximum-hour conditions and also protect the consumer against high prices. The critics of the NRA idea insist that a complex series of controls must lead to one central co-ordinating control, i.e., to some sort of dictatorship over industry. They insist that you can't "plan" production in a vacuum—*that you must plan at a price in relation to purchasing power*. In other words, unless you know in advance just how many items will move off the market at a given figure you are not "planning" at all; you are just guessing. And in guessing you are limiting the supply—which is monopolistic. If you are going to "plan" everything—supply, price, purchasing power—you must be in a position to dictate to both capital and labor, and you must, within limits, be able to coerce the choice of the consumer as he wonders whether to save, or to buy lollipops, gin, or a new car. Some labor leaders tend to go along with the Richberg school on the theory that any regulatory body under Roosevelt and the Democratic Party would inevitably consult labor's desires. The argument is that wages must be kept up if the purchasing power is to be on tap to move the planned output at the planned price.

Still another group in Washington, headed by Senator O'Mahoney of Wyoming, thinks that federal licensing of corporations is the answer. To those who shout "fascism" when this is suggested, Senator O'Mahoney points to the British Companies Act to prove that centralized control of business licensing is entirely compatible with free parliamentary institutions. And to those who shout "violation of states' rights," he remarks that Delaware and New Jersey have no "right" to define the terms on which a corporation can do business in Montana or Texas. But federal licensing would be no panacea in itself. The question would immediately be raised: Licensing for what? And the quarrel about concentration of wealth and price rigidity would begin all over again the minute Congress started to define the types of abuse that could lead to revocation of license.

The Henderson school, being pragmatic, is willing to move in numerous directions at once and to make special exceptions of sick industries like coal in order to bring about workable relationships in the price structure. It is not against Henry Wallace's efforts to control farm production and farm prices as long as there is an obstinate rigidity in the industrial side of the price structure. It is willing to admit that high hourly wage rates can be a real force in making for rigidity, and it would not object to a lowering of hourly wages in the building-trades industries. If it hesitates to suggest lower hourly wages elsewhere, that is because it does not believe in the willingness of most business men to cut their profits first. It objects to the so-called "Richberg plan," not because it wants to see a cat-and-dog fight promoted in any particular business, but because "planning," no matter how nobly motivated, is not compatible with the free market that it thinks necessary to the continuance of capitalism. But it would permit "planning" in so far as it relates to making rules for governing such things as the financing of installment buying, or the leveling out of the peaks and valleys in employment in seasonal industries.

The Henderson school has had the ear of the President—the creation of TNEC to study price movements in the U. S. economy proves that. And the Henderson program has had the attention of the Messrs. Corcoran and Cohen, who are Brandeis men from away back. The Jackson-Henderson-Corcoran "well-integrated group"—to use Raymond Moley's phrase once more —continues to push its long-term campaign of encirclement to achieve objectives that should be dear to the heart of everyone who really believes in the system of democratic capitalism. Already the holding company is on its way out in the electrical utility business. Bills are pending in Congress to make funds available at easy-money rates to medium-sized, locally-managed enterprise. And in Thurman Arnold the Department of Justice has the first vigorous trust-buster in history.

If the New Deal manages to keep control of the

Half Steel, Half Putty

Democratic Party and win the election, the second engagement will probably be fought over the question of "streamlining" the anti-trust laws. The streamlining might be designed to throw the burden of proof on industry, not the government. If such things as identical bidding, "price leadership," or lower prices for exports exist in an industry, the companies involved might be directed to "show cause" and prove social justification for their price tactics. Prosecution of offending companies might be made more simple by cutting down the opportunities for intermediate court appeals.

Still another engagement may be fought on the patent-law front. As they now stand, the patent laws are so stringent that industry itself has had in many cases to adopt the self-protective practice of pooling its patents. New Dealers would like to revise the laws in such a way that the inventor would continue to get his royalties while *all* industrialists get a crack at the use of the invention.

If Leon Henderson and his friends have not been averse to hinting at coercion, they hope nonetheless that it will not be necessary to ask for restrictive legislation. They trust that heavy industry will see its own interest in a sensitive pricing policy. But in case the appeal to self-interest in the basic industries fails, there is always the taxing power. Some radical New Dealers have talked about a tax to hit directly at size in industries where Big Ones, or Big Twos, or Big Threes are able to administer prices simply by naming their own prices. If you tax bigness, these New Dealers have argued, you will force uneconomic units to dissolve into their constituent parts. The more companies you have in a given field, so they say, the more chance you have of getting one competitive maverick such as Henry Ford—or E. T. Weir of the depression epoch —to make things interesting. If a tax on bigness is in the cards, it would probably be on net income *before* interest on funded debt. Their idea here would be not to penalize companies with a small bonded indebtedness or none at all.

But in hinting at a tax on bigness, the radical New Dealers know that they are moving onto ground that is politically very dangerous. Besides, bigness sometimes promotes efficiency, and a blanket tax might prove discriminatory. As I have said, the radical New Dealers would prefer to see big industries set their own houses in order. They would prefer to see them lower prices, and take the cut out of dividends, not out of labor. In arguing for cheapness at the expense of profits, not wages, they are not selling out to Karl Marx, as their more vociferous opponents would have it. Actually, they are taking their stand on the great conservative economic Bible, Adam Smith's "Wealth of Nations." Said Adam Smith at the dawn of the modern era: "In reality high profits tend much more to raise the price of work [i.e., final price of goods] than high wages." And: "In a country which had acquired its full complement of riches, where in every particular branch of business there was the greatest quantity of stock that could be employed in it, as the ordinary rate of clear profit would be very small, so the usual market rate of interest which could be afforded out of it would be so low as to render it impossible for any but the very wealthiest people to live upon the interest of their money." The radical New Dealers—who insist they are the true conservatives—ask the men who call themselves conservatives to ponder these words and learn something about the way a conservative, competitive capitalist system is supposed to work.

As a matter of fact, the radical New Dealers aren't asking the conservatives to take a loss. Flexible prices in any one industry may mean lowered profits. But if prices were flexible throughout the entire economic system, depressions, so the New Dealers argue, would be short and sharp—on the 1921 model, rather than long and draggingly painful, as in 1930-1933. Under flexibility, profits might actually be greater in the long run, and securities might therefore be worth more. It is to capitalist self-interest, not to socialist hopes, that the Henderson school is making its appeal.

CHAPTER VII

Growing Points

IN ENGLAND, land of the mock turtle and the gryphon, there used to be a creature known as the Chesterbelloc. Presumably the head of the beast was the head of Hilaire Belloc, while the body, as might be guessed, was the ponderous carcass of Gilbert Chesterton. The Chesterbelloc carried the banner for a mode of economic life known as distributivism, or distributism. The interest of the Chesterbelloc in distributism grew out of its preoccupation with the life of the Catholic Middle Ages—a perhaps romanticized time when England was, in Belloc's grave language, "an England of the fields." The distributive state, according to Belloc, is a "third form of state," neither capitalist (which Belloc makes synonymous with the modern system under which most people work for wages) nor servile (under which heading Belloc lumps every form of security-state from that of the Greek and Oriental tyrants to the communism of Josef Stalin). In the distributive state, "the families composing it are, in a determining number, owners of the land and the means of production as well as themselves the human agents of production. . . ." The Chesterbelloc's crusade for this admittedly primitive form of society was based on

228

moral rather than on economic grounds: distributism, argued Belloc, "gives freedom: that is, the exercise of one's will." To the end that freedom as the "exercise of one's will" might be maintained, the Chesterbelloc was prepared to sacrifice many of the benefits (and the insecurity, as well) of modern capitalist production.

To an England that had practically destroyed its agriculture in its push toward specializing as the workshop of the nineteenth-century world, the program of the Chesterbelloc seemed nonsensical, even faddish. Simply because it lacked a native soil on the tight little island, distributism could grow there only as a cult. The cult may have made fundamental sense; but the fact remained that cults are seldom, if ever, effective. In America, when distributism was taken up by Mr. Seward Collins several years ago, it seemed almost as literary and unreal as the New Humanism—especially so in view of Mr. Collins' animosity toward the various American radical movements stemming from Populism. Americans didn't have to go to the Chesterbelloc for a faddish program and propaganda of decentralized small ownership; they had a whole vital tradition of Jeffersonian democracy from which they could draw "distributist" inspiration. Nevertheless, they followed Mr. Collins in preferring faddish sources to native philosophers such as Jefferson, Henry George or John Taylor of Caroline. The "Tennessee Agrarians" were not, of course, ignorant of the American Jeffersonian-Populist tradition. Yet in choosing to call themselves agrarians these boys and girls, poets and biographers for the most part, went forth to take their stand for a creed that must have seemed phony, or at least precious, to the dirt farmers of their acquaintance. It will always be a matter for ironical notation that during the period of our literary agrarianism a Marxist, Mr. Louis Hacker, was doing the most skillful investigation of the Populist platforms of the Eighties and the Nineties. From these, if from anywhere, the true milk of decentralism, or distributism, or agrarianism, may be imbibed.

If distributism had had to depend on its literary proponents, it would have died the death reserved for all social philosophies that do not spring from the grass roots. But luckily for those who hope to avoid complete capitulation to the collectivist philosophies that dominate our age, distributism still springs from the American earth. Its most impressive resurgence in recent years is to be found in the consumer co-operative movement, which has been growing steadily throughout the Thirties, in good years and bad years alike.

Most Americans still think of consumer co-operation as something practiced by the Swedes. And since the Scandinavian way of life impresses average let-well-enough-alone Americans as too good to be true, they think of the co-operative movement as vaguely Utopian. They tend to lump it with Technocracy and its dream of engineer samurai, or with Major C. H.

Douglas's Social Credit. American panacea addicts have done nothing to dispel this general belief; a few years ago these starry-eyed folk were busy boning up on Swedish grammar and getting ready to sail for Stockholm to investigate a "middle way" they might have found in their own backyard. In 1936, at the height of the Scandinavian "middle way" furore, some 2,000,000 U. S. families, most of them in farm areas, were already saving themselves money by doing co-operative buying. The same number is still doing co-operative buying in 1940—only more of it.

The technique of this buying has its variations and complexities, but fundamentally it is simple enough. If you are interested in getting the benefits of co-operative purchasing, you organize a group to put up the necessary capital. Then you rent a store and hire a store manager. Through him you buy the goods you need at wholesale and sell them to yourself at retail. At the end of the year you pay the accrued surplus back to yourself in the form of a rebate according to your volume of purchases. In this way you save money that otherwise goes to outside stockholders or into big salaries or into advertising.

American co-operators have already organized some 6,500 retail consumer co-operatives. Under a sort of reverse holding-company control, these have in turn set up twenty-six big regional wholesale co-operatives, which buy from factories and sell to the retail co-ops to which they rebate the wholesale profits. In 1939

U. S. consumer co-operatives did a gross business of $600,000,000, an increase of twenty per cent over 1936. And because the movement threatens to spread from the farm to urban areas, the chain stores and the large and small retail merchants have been looking at consumer co-operation with uneasy eyes. They don't know quite what it portends but they are vaguely aware that it may not bode them good.

Technocracy's *sine qua non* was the "seizure of power" by the engineers; Social Credit, less cosmic in its conception, merely demanded the seizure of the Treasury and the banking system by the social cred- iteers whether they knew it or not. There is nothing so thrilling about Consumer Co-operation, which neces- sarily begins at home with the local community. Take, for instance, the mid-1930 experience of Madison and Summit, two New Jersey suburban towns. These towns are certainly not proletarian; neither are they *haut ton*. They are populated largely with white collar and pro- fessional people whose average family income is some- where around $2,500 a year. Some of them are teachers at Drew University, a small Methodist college in Madison. Others are researchers and technicians em- ployed in the Bell Telephone laboratories at Summit or on West Street in New York, across the Hudson River.

Teachers and technicians had listened to orators in boiled shirts who talked about the "doom of the price system." But meanwhile the price system could not be evaded; Madison and Summit people had to pay their bills. And their incomes did not go up in 1933 and 1934 as prices rose under the vitalizing wand of Franklin D. Roosevelt. Without knowing anything about the Swedish, Finnish, Danish, and British co-operatives, the teachers and technicians began to feel their way toward Consumer Co-operation. There was no talk of a new world; they were interested in making current and inelastic incomes buy more goods.

The first thing they did was to locate an efficiently operated independent coal mine at Pittston, Pennsylvania, and get a favorable price quoted at the pit head. Then they hired a truck. The truck brought back the coal, delivered each separate order to its individual coalbin—and the buyers discovered they had saved $1 to $2 a ton by cutting out most of the middleman's services. That was in 1934. In the summer of 1935 the Madison and Summit consumers, now having a joint membership of 134 families, opened a co-operative store at Chatham, which is midway between the two towns. Paid-in capital amounted to $400, half of which was spent for a dilapidated delivery truck, the rest for store equipment, goods and the first week's salary of $22 for a manager. The New Jersey Consumers' Co-operative, Inc., had officially been born. By the end of 1936 NJCC—co-operators, like New Dealers, love to use initials—discovered that it had done a gross business of $40,000, and its membership had increased to 398 families. And a housewife who had spent $360 in the co-operative got a rebate of around $14 on her purchases.

To those persons who make enough to pay an appreciable income tax, the sum of $14 a year may seem trifling, the game of co-operation not worth the candle. But the story of the initial growth of NJCC is typical, for consumer co-operatives in urban or suburban areas usually begin with buying clubs organized by white-collar or professional people to whom $14 bulks large in terms of new clothes, new shoes, or just a weekend jaunt to the seashore.

The pattern for effective consumer co-operation was set in 1844 by twenty-eight English weavers of Rochdale, a sooty town in the heart of the Lancashire textile district that gave the world its first and grisliest sweat-shops. In the decade that is known to English history as "the hungry Forties" the Rochdale men, women, and children worked from six in the morning to eight at night for the piddling wage of one or tuppence an hour. Some of the mill hands made as little as twenty-five pence a week. England was then simmering with the agitation of the Chartist movement, whose orators went up and down the land calling on the Queen's Ministers to take note of the degraded lot of the workingman. But while the weavers of Rochdale were waiting for Parliament to act they had—like the New Jersey suburbanites of ninety years later—to meet their expenses.

Accordingly they pooled their capital—twenty-eight

hard-earned pounds, a pound for each member—and rented a poor make-shift shop in Toad Lane and stocked it with foodstuffs bought at wholesale. Cut-rate co-operatives had often collapsed for want of working capital, so the Toad Lane store made it a principle to charge the going market retail price. Business was done on a strictly cash basis. At the year's end, if there was anything left over after reserves for expansion and education had been set aside, the surplus was rebated to the customer member in proportion to his purchases. A customer might buy more than one share of stock in the enterprise and he might get 5 per cent on his invested capital in addition to the money received in rebates, but no matter whether he owned one share of stock or fifty he got only one vote. This insured democratic control from the bottom up, and this method of control is what leads propagandistic writers on co-operation to speak of the movement as the middle way between communism and fascism.

In the ninety-three years since the shop in Toad Lane opened its doors to sell its first pitiful supply of flour, sugar, butter, and oatmeal, the co-operatives that have stuck to Rochdale principles have grown and prospered, while the ones that have departed from them—say, to extend credit to their members—have almost without exception gone on the rocks. The suburban co-operators of Madison and Summit might have joined the failures if it hadn't been for the literature of the Co-operative League of the U. S. A., a propagandizing organization set up in 1916 by a socially-minded surgeon, Dr. James Peter Warbasse. Through this literature the Jerseyites became well acquainted with the story of Rochdale. They learned some astonishing things as well. In their innocence they had felt rather alone when they started their venture in cooperation. But the League brought them news that thousands of other Americans were cutting the cost of living by the Rochdale method.

League pamphlets and speakers told them, for example, about the Finns of northern Minnesota, Wisconsin, and Michigan who had been co-operating since before the First World War. In 1939 the pioneer Finnish retail co-operative—the one in Cloquet, Minnesota—did close to $1,200,000 worth of business in groceries, flour, feed, hardware, building materials, farm machinery, drygoods, clothes, shoes, furniture, household appliances, and oil and gas. The Finns had organized their own Central Co-operative Wholesale at Superior, Wisconsin, as a centralized buying agency for the district retail co-operatives in 1917; this wholesale served as a prototype for twenty-five other large wholesales that have since been organized throughout the country. Half a million farmers of the Middle West—preponderantly in Indiana, Ohio, Illinois, Kansas, Nebraska, Michigan, Minnesota, Wisconsin, and the Dakotas—use these wholesales to buy their feeds, fertilizers, binder twine, gasoline, and oil on a

Rochdale basis. Up in Ithaca, New York, the Grange League Federation—a farmers' purchasing association —did $44,000,000 worth of business in 1938.

Just as the Madison and Summit suburbanites were discovering the existence of a co-operative movement in America, the U. S. as a whole began to hear of Sweden, Finland, and Denmark, where consumer co-operatives had boomed all throughout the Twenties. People had been introduced to a nebulous creature called "the consumer" in 1933, when a Consumers' Advisory Board was set up within the NRA with the late Mrs. Mary Harriman Rumsey in charge, and when Dr. Frederic C. Howe, a stanch old war horse of the pre-War Progressive movement, was named Consumers' Counsel of the AAA. But the habitat of this creature was unspecified. And it was soon apparent that Mrs. Rumsey and Dr. Howe were largely powerless to discover his whereabouts; NRA and AAA were frankly dedicated to the producer interests of the U. S. Of far greater importance in making the U. S., and particularly U. S. liberals, consumer-conscious was Marquis W. Childs, an alert newspaperman in the Washington bureau of the St. Louis *Post-Dispatch*. Childs had visited Sweden at the suggestion of his managing editor, O. K. Bovard, and had written some Sunday articles on the Swedish co-operatives. Hopefully, he expanded these into a book, "Sweden: The Middle Way." The Yale University Press took a chance on it, publishing it early in 1936, and to the astonishment of everyone concerned it leaped to the position of best seller almost at once. Before the year was over it had sold 22,000 copies.

The most effective copy was the one with the marked passages that a civic-minded New Yorker, one Robert J. Caldwell, put into the hands of President Roosevelt in Florida. Presumably the President read it with rapt attention. For when Axel Wenner-Gren, maker of the Electrolux refrigerator, was visiting at the White House, Mr. Roosevelt, aware of his guest's Scandinavian origin, turned the conversation to consumer co-operatives. What did Mr. Wenner-Gren think of them? Mr. Wenner-Gren thought a lot of them; he said they were the things that would save capitalism.

The President leaped to this like a schoolboy hearing the recess bell; he called in Harry Hopkins, and a group of three was hurriedly named to study consumer co-operatives on the spot in Europe. The three were Jacob Baker, one of Harry Hopkins's WPA aides; Leland Olds, Secretary of the New York Power Authority; and Charles E. Stuart, New York engineer. The trio didn't entirely satisfy veteran co-operators, who felt that one of their number should be included, as did some of the farm organizations. And so, just to please everyone concerned, the President enlarged the commission to six by adding Clifford V. Gregory, editor of the Prairie Farmer; Robin Hood, secretary of the National Co-operative Council; and Miss Emily C. Bates of Kansas City.

The President was, of course, sincerely interested in finding out the exact scope and nature of the co-operative movement in northern Europe. But to Jim Farley the commission meant something else again; it served as an excellent temporizing device to get the subject of consumer co-operation off the Democratic agenda until after the 1936 election. Jim had been receiving frightened letters from small retailers and he knew the whole thing was loaded with political dynamite. Hence, the story goes, when Senator Wagner went to Philadelphia with a co-operative plank in his pocket he was told to keep it there; the matter would not be ripe for discussion until the President's commission had returned from abroad.

When the commission did come home after a Summer of looking at stores, bakeries, margarine and electric-light bulb factories, modernistic housing developments, and all the other aspects of consumer co-operation, they were already differing about opinions and recommendations. However, the six members were pretty well agreed as to the main facts, although the statistics that they had to accept were roughly arrived at since no government agencies have made authoritative surveys of co-operative trade. In Sweden, the country that had received the most publicity in the U. S., the co-operatives did only an estimated 10 per cent of the total retail trade, but the co-operators had succeeded in breaking cartel monopoly prices in such things as margarine, galoshes, and electric-light bulbs by going into the manufacturing business for themselves. This is what has made the Swedish co-operative movement so spectacular. In Denmark, Finland, and England the co-operators had been less startling but more pervasive. Around 15 per cent of the retail business of Denmark is co-operatively done; in Finland the figure is 35 per cent; in England, 15 per cent. These figures need some refinement to give them meaning. In England, for example, 50 per cent of the population buys in the co-operative stores. This 50 per cent accounts for only 15 per cent of the retail business for a simple reason: it is the relatively poor lower middle class that belongs to the co-operatives.

The figure of 15 per cent for the co-operative retail trade of Denmark gives no true reflection of how co-operative-minded the Danes are. For Denmark is also a country of co-operative agricultural marketing and processing associations—all of them organized for the benefit of producers. Any producers' co-operative is necessarily interested in making money for its members, whether by pooling shipments to save freight costs or cutting down on production when an oversupply of the goods it sells threatens to demoralize the market. Its interests are thus, in nine cases out of ten, diametrically opposed to the desire of the consumer for cheapness. In Denmark, however, a unique situation exists: man as a producer does not war unduly with man as a consumer. Denmark has a large exportable agricultural surplus. The Danish farmer—and he is one-third of the population—wins both ways: he sells most of his dairy products abroad through his producers' co-operative at the highest price obtainable; then he turns around and buys imported manufactured goods at a consumer co-operative.

Since the United States has a complex, high-order, continent-wide capitalistic economy, its problems naturally differ from those of the bucolic countries of northern Europe. They even differ from those of England, which is a nation largely without farmers. For these reasons President Roosevelt took no action on the report of his European commission. His attitude was that consumer co-operation is something that must start with the consumer, where he feels he needs it, and not with Congress. About all the government can do for consumer co-operatives is to give the idea publicity, stand by as a moneylender to co-operatives that can give security, and take their side against chain stores and private retailers that want laws passed to hinder the growth of co-operatives.

All things considered, the U. S. co-operative movement has done very well to date without political aid. It is true that only a fraction of U. S. business is co-operatively conducted. And it is also true that more than 75 per cent of the co-operative business is done for a profit by marketing and producers' co-operatives such as the California Fruit Growers Exchange, the Farmers National Grain Corporation, the American

Cotton Co-operative Association, the Dairymen's League, and Land O' Lakes Creameries. That leaves the consumer co-operatives a mere 1.5 per cent of the nation's retail business—which sounds like small change. But $600,000,000, the approximate figure for 1938 consumer-co-operative business, becomes impressive when it is compared with the mere chemical trace that existed in the middle Twenties. And the sum indicates real growth when we compare it with $425,000,-000, the figure for 1935.

More important than the figures, however, is the articulation of a national pattern for consumer co-operation. Seven years ago a few of the big regional co-operative wholesales decided they needed a national wholesale to make contracts for bulk products such as oil, binder twine, feed, and fertilizer. So they set up National Co-operatives, Inc., whose present headquarters are in Chicago. In 1938 National Co-operatives did a gross purchasing business of $58,000,000. It sells electrical equipment and radios to please farmers who have joined rural-electrification co-ops. National Co-operatives is controlled by member regional wholesales. And since the regional wholesales are entirely the property of the member retails, one can liken the co-operative economic structure to the *theoretical* political structure of the Soviet Union, where the ultimate power is supposed to be vested in the village, farm and factory soviets. But there is this salient difference: the consumer co-operative movement has no political party, no bureaucracy, no boss, to negate the processes of democracy.

At its local end the co-operative movement presents a picture of increasing diversity. Farmers have always been willing to share machinery and services, but since consumer co-operation started to fan out through Minnesota and the Dakotas there has been a great increase in co-operative bull-and-stallion clubs in those states. On the U. S. campus the co-op bookstore is a venerable institution. During the middle Thirties college students adapted the idea to co-operative dormitories and eating clubs. There are Rochdale co-operative apartment houses in New York City. Co-operative medicine has largely chosen to follow the group-insurance pattern, but there is a bona fide co-operative hospital at Elk City, Oklahoma. Since the government has lent or earmarked over $250,000,000 for rural electrification, farmers in forty-four states have formed rural-electrification co-ops and have been stringing their own power lines to their own poles. The current is bought on a collective co-operative basis from existing power companies. As for co-operative banks, known as credit unions, they are one of the oldest forms of consumer co-operation in the U. S. A credit union is simply a mutual banking arrangement; you belong; you own stock; you get a credit rating after you join which enables you to borrow up to a fixed limit at a low rate of interest. Since their start in 1908, the number of U. S. credit unions has grown to 8,500, with an estimated membership of 2,225,000. The Municipal Credit Union of New York City has assets of $2,500,000.

Historically, the co-operative movement can be best understood by following the various local and regional trickles that have flowed together to make up the national co-operative stream. The pioneer Rochdale in the U. S. was opened in 1845, but the first trickle of importance was started by the Finns of Wisconsin, Minnesota, and northern Michigan before U. S. entry into the First World War.

The Finns had gone into the woods of Minnesota, Wisconsin, and Michigan around 1890 as sawmill hands and lumberjacks—jobs they had known in the old country. But unlike the Yankee lumbermen who followed the trail of the falling pine to Oregon and the Pacific Coast, they stayed on to farm a country of burned stumps, flinty uplands, and poor, peaty valley soil. A clannish folk, the Finns kept to their own language and read the newspapers that friends mailed them from far-off Helsingfors. Finland was then part of Russia; it had been marked out by the Czar's Ministers for complete Russification. And as part of the Russification drive the Finns were forbidden to meet in patriotic or in social organizations. They were, however, permitted two modes of congregation: one, in church; the other, in trade associations.

So the Finns in the homeland organized themselves

into co-operatives for the double purpose of saving money and sneaking in a little general conversation about the iniquities of the Czar. And the Finns of the U. S., meeting at the crossroads of the North, chattered eagerly about the movement across the sea. There was more than sentiment in their proposals to imitate the home folks. In the first place, the Finns have a passion for their own breadstuffs: *hapan reikaleipa* (sour whole rye), *skreadlimppu* (yeast bread). And they pined for thick, heavy smoked and pickled meats. Yankee store-keepers couldn't believe these desires were either legitimate or lasting, and so the Yankees lost the grocery trade to the new Finnish co-operatives.

The most vigorous pioneer unit in the Finnish Northwest was the Minnesota Cloquet Stock Mercantile Company, started in 1910 with 110 members. Today, in a town of 7,000 people, the Cloquet company (now called the Cloquet Co-operative Society) has a membership of 2,500 families, employs sixty-five persons, has a monthly payroll of $6,000, keeps nine trucks busy, and has three branch stores. It also has an auditorium, a library, and functions as a social club and town hall as well as an economic institution.

The effects of Cloquet pioneering can be seen all over northern Minnesota, Wisconsin, and Michigan. With four other co-operatives, Cloquet set up the Trico Co-operative Oil Association in 1929. Trico's two bulk stations and five tank trucks serve three counties; its $10,000 filling station on the main street of Cloquet is one of the sights of the town. To the north of Cloquet, in the opencut mining country of the Mesabi, local consumer co-operatives have formed the Mesabi Range Co-operative Federation at Virginia, Minnesota, and have branched out into production by starting their own sausage factory. At Duluth, Minnesota, and Superior, Wisconsin, where the great ore boats dock, Finns, Swedes, and Hungarians run their own co-operative boardinghouses—chiefly because they agree in their tastes for heavy foods. Many of the northern co-operatives own shares in the Co-operative Park Association at Brule, Wisconsin, where co-operators camp, fish, and swim at cheap rates in the summer.

In 1917 the U. S. was on rations; it was Hooverizing on sugar, meat, wheat products. Co-operative retailers felt the pinch; they claimed that jobbers who had only a limited allotment of foodstuffs were discriminating against them. The Finns of Cloquet decided then and there to organize their own co-operative wholesale. With delegates from eighteen other co-operative stores they met at Superior. A collection of $15.50 was raised, and with this initial working capital the Central Co-operative Wholesale came into being. By the end of 1938 the investment amounted to more than $219,000. Ninety per cent of this had been built up out of patronage refund money that member retail societies chose to leave untouched.

In the beginning the Central Co-operative Wholesale acted as a jobber, buying its goods from other

246

wholesales. Today it has its own bakery, its own coffee-roasting plant. It makes its outside purchases directly from packers and manufacturers and distributes many of its goods under the registered CO-OP trademark. Its training school teaches young co-operators store management, cost accounting, and double-entry book-keeping. Nearly 500 have attended the courses, and you can find Central Co-op graduates in key co-operative jobs in many parts of the U. S.

After the Finns, came the American farmer to swell the stream of consumer co-operation, but not until other tactics and other strategies had failed. Since the American farmer has been primarily a business man, completely producer-minded, those strategies were concerned with running his farm for profit. With the collapse of farm prices after the War, he tried to get the government to buy his surplus at an artificial price. And he also turned an ear to the evangelistic Aaron Sapiro of San Francisco, who toured the country with the gospel of the producers' co-operative and co-operative marketing association.

Farm leaders had gone abroad in 1923 with a commission to study the European co-operative movement, but Mr. Sapiro's eloquence kept them from seeing the consumer end of that development; and marketing associations sprang up in his path. Not until those associations proved impotent to check the fall of prices did the farmers finally (around 1926) turn to consumer co-operation. And even then their interest was confined to the purchase of producers' goods, i.e., goods used in the fabrication of other goods. The business of the big farm purchasing co-operatives of the Dakotas, Wisconsin, Minnesota, Michigan, Kansas, Missouri, Indiana, Illinois, Ohio, Pennsylvania, and New York is largely in oil and gasoline (for use in the farmer's trucks and tractors); in stock feed and fertilizer; in seed and in new-hatched chicks. The farmer is still thinking as a business man and he has discovered that consumers' co-operation in buying producers' goods is a good business tactic.

Idealists in the co-operative movement don't like to stress this. But the statistics stress it. The figure for total consumer co-operative business in 1938 was $600,000,000; the total done by the big farm purchasing associations for the same year was $440,000,000. Some of this was spent on consumers' goods, of course. And some of the oil and gasoline bought from the co-operatives went to take the farmer's car on pleasure trips. But most of the money was spent in the interests of production for profit. There are three times as many purchasing associations handling petroleum products and stock feed as there are handling groceries. The big regional wholesales exist mostly for the centralized purchasing of producers' goods. For example, the Grange League Federation of Ithaca, New York, which did a $44,000,000 business in the 1938 season, bought feed, seed, hay, twine, paint, fertilizer, lime, coal, and sprays for its 80,000 members. Only the coal and the paint can properly be called consumers' goods —and the chances are that most of the paint went on barns and chicken houses before the farmer got around to painting the old homestead. In the vast shuffle of producers' goods the popular picture of the housewife going to the co-operative grocery store and saving 4 per cent on the annual food bill tends to get lost. Consistent with the American character, consumer co-operation turns out to be, not a way of life, but a way of running the purchasing department of a business concern.

Since the Finns pioneered in U. S. co-operatives it is significant that few Finns are numbered among the conspicuous leaders of the movement today. The reason is that Finnish co-operation is an expression of upwelling community spirit. The native U. S. variety is, on the other hand, the paradoxical creation of vigorous individualists. There is Ed Babcock, for instance, an imperious breaker of hunting and jumping horses who runs the Grange League Federation of Ithaca "from the top down." He has not seen fit to make the Grange co-op over into a pure and simple Rochdale by placing its voting control in the hands of the members, and so it differs from the middle-western wholesale co-operatives.

The leaders of the midwest co-operatives are more trustful of democracy. But even they have not waited for the masses to reach decisions; instead, they have gone out and sold their ideas to sometimes reluctant followers. The Consumers' Co-operative Association of North Kansas City, which ships oil and gas, farm supplies, and groceries to 313 member societies in eight states, was built up through the single-minded devotion of Howard A. Cowden, a lean, six-foot Missouri idealist. Edwin Galiton Cort was the earnest individual who put over the first of the big co-op oil wholesales in the U. S., the Midland Co-operative Wholesale of Minnesota. The Indiana co-operative movement would most likely have been swallowed up in bankruptcy if Isaac Harvey Hull, a bald, rotund Hoosier, hadn't come along to rescue it by turning it to Rochdale principles.

Able as all these men are, however, none of them approaches the record of Murray D. Lincoln, of Ohio. Some fourteen years ago Lincoln quit a good job with the late Myron Herrick's Cleveland bank to go to work for the Ohio Farm Bureau. Like the other Lincoln, Murray is tall and gangling. At first he was under the spell of the Sapiro philosophy and thought producers' and marketing co-operatives were the way out for the farmer. But none of the producers' co-operatives that he had a hand in organizing were effective in raising farm prices. Lincoln had gone to Europe with the co-operative-inspection junket of 1923, and in 1926 he decided to give the consumer co-operation he had seen abroad a try.

Born on a farm in east Massachusetts, Lincoln had worked as a government county farm agent before Banker Herrick picked him to drum up a business in farm loans. When he saw the cream of the Ohio farmer's profits being funneled into the bank via high interest rates, he resolved to help the farmer attain some measure of financial independence. So his first act as a farm-bureau consumer co-operator was to form an automobile-insurance company to write insurance at lower rates for farmers, and also to build up credit reserves to finance a broad-scale co-operative program. That program eventually resulted in a Farm Bureau Credit Corporation, through which Ohio farmers can now borrow at a low rate of interest for anything connected with farm operation but the purchase of real estate.

In urban-industrial districts consumer co-operation among workers has been rare. And where it does exist there are special reasons for it. Racial solidarity among immigrant groups is the most important special reason. In Maynard and Fitchburg, Massachusetts, and in Brooklyn Finnish workers have co-operated successfully for years. The Bohemian co-operative in Dillonvale, Ohio, has grown in its thirty years from a buying club of ten families into a prosperous business. Since the depression the Negroes of the North have learned of consumer co-operation. Negro "bury leagues" have existed ever since Reconstruction in the South, but the principle of cutting the cost of dying was never applied by them to the cost of living until some unemployed Negro steelworkers of Gary, Indiana, led by a Negro schoolteacher, started a buying club in 1932. The buying club became a store and in 1935 it was doing a business of $35,000.

Anglo-Saxon urban Americans have been slower to co-operate, but there are examples of town consumer co-operatives that transcend racial lines. In Flint, Michigan, eight men read Justice Louis D. Brandeis's "Other People's Money" in 1934 and the result was a consumers' co-operative of 260 families. In New York City the Amalgamated Clothing Workers have a co-operative apartment house development in the Van Cortlandt Park region. And New York white-collar and professional people have patronized the cafeterias of Consumers' Co-operative Services, Inc., ever since 1920.

There are a number of regional leagues for co-operative promotion, most of them attached to regional co-operative wholesales. But the chief unifying agent in the country is the Co-operative League of the U. S. A., from whose small, red brick headquarters at 167 West Twelfth Street in New York there pours a steady stream of co-operative literature and speakers. For years the founder, Dr. Warbasse, supported the league out of his own pocket and did most of the proselytizing; his insignificant goatee and thin white hair were seen up and down the land wherever consumer co-operators were meeting in sparse convention. Today the league has for its energetic secretary Eugene R. Bowen, who quit building power farm machinery to publicize co-operation. He has made the league into a high-powered publicity center. Affiliated with it are most of the big regional wholesales in the U. S. and it is also tied in with the International Co-operative Alliance of London.

The Co-operative League steers clear of loaded words, of picking and choosing between various Utopian ideals for co-operators. But under the official surface the movement naturally reflects struggling philosophies. There are the well-meaning liberals whose chief contribution is talk; they will move on to the next world-saving panacea when the topical flavor of co-operation has been exhausted. There are Left-wingers among the Finns who look on the Ohio and Indiana co-operators as suspect. Some of the co-operators think of the movement as an all-embracing life, something which, if pursued to its logical conclusion, would result in the peaceful supersession of capitalism by a socialism far more democratic than that of the Soviet Union.

They argue that if every ultimate consumer bought everything he used at a retail co-operative and received the accrued surplus back at the year end in the form of rebates, there would obviously be no profit left in the retail trade. Manufacturers selling to the co-operative wholesales would, however, still be making a profit. But the wholesales could put an end to this by building their own factories. The end result would be that people would merely produce and perform services and receive produce and services in exchange. Capitalism would thus be subtly transformed into "production for use," a sort of glorified barter, with money functioning solely as a medium of exchange. But not even the most hopeful—or radical—of American co-operators will argue that any such Utopia is on the blueprints for the next ten or twenty years. They are satisfied to take the current cash benefits of co-operation and let Utopia follow if it will.

In its immediate day-to-day aspects, consumer co-operation strikes at monopoly prices, intensifies competition, and actually limbers up the capitalist system in areas where it has a substantial foothold. Inasmuch as it returns its surplus to the small consumer, whose needs are so great that he is almost certain to go out and spend the money again for more commodities, it tends to keep capital from agglomerating, from being funneled off into the pockets of wealthy stockholders who do not spend it for consumers' goods. Thus if the movement grew to national proportions its effect would be to rob the New York investment market of money that might go into needless plant expansion or stock gambling. Co-operators claim that a well-developed co-operative program would act as a brake on such orgies as 1929.

But there is a question as to how far the co-operative movement can go outside the farm areas. Co-operators are leery of organized politics; they think they have found "the economic solution to a social problem." The history of Germany, Italy, and Japan proves that economics, even the economics of consumer co-operation, are not enough to preserve democracy. Both Germany and Italy had numbers of Rochdale co-operatives before Hitler and Mussolini substituted state for democratic control. And even under democracy the purely economic approach isn't enough. Successful consumer co-operation lowers the cost of living, yes. But where political or social pressure doesn't interpose arbitrary restraining factors, the wage level in any given area tends to fall where living costs fall. That is elementary economic law. And where consumer co-operation is the means of cutting the cost of living it can be used by industrialists as an excuse for wage cuts. Thus the co-operator can be robbed of his gains. Knowing this, Marquis Childs has warned U. S. consumers that they had better imitate England and supplement the co-operative movement with a labor movement designed to preserve gains in living standards. And legislation to preserve these gains is, of course, a matter of politics.

The most immediate threat to the growth of consumer co-operation is competition from the chain stores, which have lusty leadership and funds with which to fight. Since the chain stores save so much money by buying in bulk, they can presumably afford to slash prices below what they are now. This is almost certain to slow up any Rochdale advance in populous communities where co-operative buying is not sufficiently large to compete against rigorous price cutting and the careful spreading of loss-leader bait.

The American Stakes

Since the co-operative movement doesn't have to advertise, it can always expect some antagonism from the more venal section of the press. And since the movement is necessarily an enemy of the expensively maintained and nationally promoted brands in groceries, soaps, tires, and medicines, it should encounter at least some hostility on the part of the big packers, canners, and manufacturers.

Finally, there is the barrier of heavy industry. Should consumer co-operation feel that it must work backward and organize the production of its own automobiles and steel girders to keep itself from being mulcted, it would eventually come up against the brutal fact of ownership. The major raw materials are not to be had except from private owners who demand a certain price for parting with them. It would cost co-operative car builders just as much money to buy steel from E. T. Weir or Eugene Grace as it now costs General Motors or Chrysler. It might even cost more.

Because of these stubborn facts, consumer co-operation can hardly expect to reach Utopia tomorrow. But when one reflects that the movement has barely got a toehold in the U. S. it is not much of a prophecy to risk that it will have a substantial growth before running up against a stone wall. After all, we can go back to the fact that the English consumer co-operatives do 15 per cent of the retail business of the country, while the American consumer co-operatives do only a little more than 1.5 per cent.

The chances are that a co-operative retail business of, say, 5 per cent in the U. S. would still leave the A & P, Standard Brands, and General Foods some margin of profit. So long as the profit margin remains, the co-operative enemy can count on some quarter, at least. In point of fact if co-operation can double its business in five years it will be happy. From 1.5 to 3 per cent doesn't sound like much, but it is still an increase of 100 per cent.

Both marketing and consumer co-operation have been mistaken for socialism. Actually, they depend largely on the existence and preservation of an antecedent individualism—on owners of productive land and equipment with money to spend. They are techniques to be used by small owners, not the essence of the distributist, or decentralist, philosophy. To preserve the essence of individualism is the hope of at least ninety per cent of the American people: nearly all of us want a more completely distributist, or decentralist, economic and social system. But only one man in America seems bent on moving mountains to get there. That man is Mr. Ralph Borsodi, a consulting economist who has an almost anarchist prejudice against the institution of the State. Borsodi was one of the first economists to see that the savings effected by mass production tended to be eaten up by the costs which necessarily include the "waste" of mass advertising. Other economists have taken off from this point to plump for socialist plan-

257

ning. But not so Borsodi, who flatly argues that the problem of distribution is essentially insoluble in either modern capitalist or socialist society. In a modern capitalist state competition between corporations results in the wastes of mass advertising and the progressive adulteration of goods; in a collectivist state the competition of various government "trusts" for raw materials and transportation rights necessitates control from the top, which is an invitation to political dictatorship over most of the tastes of the community. To solve the "insoluble," Borsodi gave a new twist to the distributism of Chesterton and Belloc: he evolved a program of largely *mechanized* home production that is designed to bring consumer and producer together in a single spot. To the people who failed to investigate Mrs. Borsodi's streamlined house, where the electrically operated gadget reigns supreme, or Mr. Borsodi's garden, which includes the wheel hoe, all this sounded like romantic medievalism involving a return to a handicraft society; it conjured up visions of backbreaking toil, of long hours digging in manure or slaving over the stove. They forgot that the medieval cottage lacked the Merryway mixer and the pressure cooker. And when Mr. Borsodi wrote his "This Ugly Civilization" and "Flight from the City," the editorial paragraphers on the metropolitan dailies shook their heads and said, "Pity poor Mrs. Borsodi." The implication was that here was just another fanatic who would disappear after making his little splash.

Borsodi, however, combines a lot of horse sense with a fanatic's will; he is a first-rate cost accountant as well as a dreamer. At Dayton, Ohio, in the early years of the depression, some public-spirited citizens under-wrote a Homestead Unit designed to match indigent men and women with small plots of land and the opportunity to build houses, to raise vegetables and poultry and to produce clothes for themselves. In look-ing for a consulting economist for the Dayton project, the sponsors naturally turned to Mr. Borsodi, whose clientele has included such hard-headed capitalist estab-lishments as Macy's. When the Subsistence Homestead Division was later organized in Washington under Secretary of the Interior Harold Ickes, Borsodi recom-mended that the $25,000,000 allocated for homestead-colonization purposes be put under the control of local organizations acting an the advice of the state universi-ties. The Dayton project was studied by the Subsistence Homestead Division—and a first loan of $50,000 was made. This was followed by allocation of $309,000 for four more Dayton units.

According to Mr. Borsodi, all was going well in Dayton until Secretary Ickes ordered the "federaliz-ing" of all projects under his control. With federal employees running back and forth between Dayton and Washington and dictating all moves of the homestead-ers in accordance with governmental red tape, the project speedily lost interest for Borsodi, who was looking for the proof of an individualist's pudding in the individualist's eating thereof. But Borsodi had got a glimpse of something in Dayton—and he started in forthwith to translate his vision into action.

Right at this point the commonsensical Borsodi triumphed over the fanatic. An old-fashioned prophet would have started a community open only to disciples who promised to do all their own gardening, canning, poultry-raising, beekeeping, goat-milking, sheep-shearing, weaving and what-not. Penalty for failure to live up to the self-sufficiency agenda would have been forfeit and expulsion. But Borsodi realized people weren't like that: the average American likes to feel he is part of the Going Concern of democratic capitalism, and is therefore content to be a wage or salary earner if possible. Being a wage earner, however, is entirely compatible with limited independence as a home-owner and possessor of garden space. With a shrewd regard for the conventional *mores*, Borsodi decided on a one-step-at-a-time program of conversion: he was looking first of all to make people home-owners, and if they could be persuaded later on to keep chickens, goats and bees, then Borsodi would have good reason to write himself down as the first practical Messiah.

But how to enable people in the $2,500-a-year class to beat the high cost of land and financing? Borsodi noted that real-estate subdividers make a practice of buying land by the half- or quarter-section for a low price to be resold as cramped building lots at a high price. To escape this vulture that battens on unearned increment in land Borsodi formed the Independence Foundation, Inc., in 1935. This non-profit organization borrowed enough money at six per cent to purchase forty acres of farm land near Suffern, New York, about an hour's commuting distance from Times Square. And with this purchase the great adventure began.

The main object was, of course, to subdivide the forty acres into one- and two-acre homestead lots and make them available to small-income families at cost. For his basic pattern, Borsodi went back to the old land-holding system of the Chautauqua communities. Instead of buying a lot outright, the prospective home-owner became a member of an association or corporation set up to hold legal title to the entire forty acres. As a member of the association, each individual was required to pay his share of the annual taxes, incidental carrying charges and amortization. By this adaptation of group ownership to individual requirements, Borsodi cut the cost of land purchase, interest, title search, taxes and preliminary architectural and engineering fees by more than half. He also cut the cost of constructing solid homes on the association land by organizing Suffern carpenters and masons into a building guild which was prepared to sacrifice the hourly wage rates of the building trades for a more or less guaranteed annual wage. The gouging contractor was eliminated by direct bargaining between the guild and the prospective home-owner. Organized labor in the building trades may grumble at such unorthodox tactics, and there have been complaints that it amounts to sabotage of the wage scale, but Borsodi's plea is that the mechanics of his building guild have earned from $1,300 to $1,500 a year as compared to the average mechanic's annual $616.

Technically, each member of the Suffern community, which has been baptized Bayard Lane, is guaranteed full control of his own acres by the legal device of indenture. Roads, new membership applications, the rate of amortization of housing loans, anything that has to do with the group as a whole, have been put under the jurisdiction of a five-man elective board, but improvements on the separate homestead plots belong strictly to the individual family. Should an individual stand in danger of losing his job and the means of settling his debt to the association, he is given full opportunity to sell his house, his garage, his improvements on the land. But he must sell at a non-speculative price. This is a constraint on the individualism which Borsodi values, but it is necessary to prevent the real-estate shark from edging into Eden. Mutual title of land tenure, however, was adopted by Borsodi as a temporary device, not as a permanent principle. When the Suffern community has paid off its debt to the Independence Foundation, the members are at complete liberty to vote the dissolution of their association, thereby assuming traditional individual title to their land as well as to their homes. Should they do this, they would, of course, run the risk of losing the advantages of a protected residential district and the low taxes that spring from assessments based on non-speculative values. Few prophets in mankind's tattered history have ever been willing to expose their followers to such temptation. But Borsodi is thoroughgoing in his individualism: he believes people have little opportunity to develop character if they are protected against the possibility of making mistakes. Borsodi is working for a community in which the minimum, not the maximum, of co-operation is the purpose. If his Bayard Lane group at Suffern chooses to go in for consumer co-operation, or for a co-operative dairy, or for credit unions, or for a group library, that is its democratic right. If it chooses to extinguish itself, that, too, is within the purview of its liberty. But there is no compulsion either to group regimentation or to group anarchy and dissolution.

If you drive out along the Haverstraw road beyond Suffern to Bayard Lane, you will find a pretty little community of substantial houses made of field stone or solid timber that are guaranteed to last as long as any early Cape Cod house in New England. To the north of this community lies a low spur of the Ramapo Mountains; an hour's distance over the southern horizon lies Manhattan. Thus the country is available for recreation and health, the metropolis for a livelihood. The people who live at Bayard Lane are, many of them, professional people: there are bank tellers, college teachers, architects. And there are members of the Ramapo Building Guild who helped create the community and then decided to avail themselves of Mr. Borsodi's land purchase and house-owning technique.

Since the success of Bayard Lane, three similar communities have been started, one at Van Houten Fields near Nyack, another at Ringwood, New Jersey, and a third in northern Westchester. Some of the people who have chosen to live in these communities have little interest in Borsodi's theories about the productive home. Others who want to use their homesteads to supplement inadequate city salaries have turned to gardening, canning, carpentry and weaving on a part-time basis. At Bayard Lane Mr. and Mrs. Borsodi have established their School for Living: there you may take courses in everything from home bread-baking and work on the loom to the proper aging of a compost heap. The Borsodis do not advocate home production unless it actually saves money or can be tackled in a spirit of fun; but they keep rigorous accounts which show in many instances that a wife can sometimes save more of her husband's salary by gardening and canning than she can earn to supplement that salary as an office worker. Moreover, by the use of electrical devices in the home, much of the effort is made easy.

Home production pays dividends in health, too. The Borsodis have a hatred for most of our mass-produced packaged and processed foods; they even insist on grinding their own wheat. To the arguments that universal home production on the Borsodi scale would result in bankruptcy for companies like General Foods and Standard Brands, the Borsodis say, "So what?" The "universal" triumph of their ideas is a long way off; and even should it come, those individuals who would lose their jobs milling the vitamins out of wheat flour for Bunchie Crunchies would presumably get new jobs manufacturing small electrically driven milling machines for kitchen use. On balance there can be no economic loss from such change in mode of production.

With Borsodi and the co-operative movement showing the way, the decentralist, or distributist, movement in the United States gives promise of a vitality which it never had in the years when the Tennessee Agrarians were taking a literary stand in favor of small ownership. The decentralizers have started their own magazine, *Free America*, which features articles on home production, on the spread of the consumer co-operative movement, on the soil depletion that follows from large-scale mechanized agriculture. Personally, when I look at one of Mr. Borsodi's communities or listen to Mr. Borsodi complaining of the routinizing features of city life, my emotions are mixed. Bayard Lane, with its vegetable gardens, its berry patches, its fruit trees and its carpenter shop, is a picture of at least relative independence and contentment. But what can relative independence for twenty or thirty families mean in a land of 10,000,000 unemployed? What can Bayard Lane mean in a world whose economy is organized for war?

The answer is, of course, that Borsodi and the decentralists are not trying to save the world with one magical reform. They are interested for the moment in saving a few people, in the hope that the gospel will spread slowly through the years. Belloc's own criticism of the complete distributist state is still fairly sound. The distributist state must necessarily tend to technological conservatism, which makes it a natural prey to the industrial mechanization of the power-state. For a hundred years after the Great Revolution of 1789 France approximated the distributist ideal, with the result that she fell behind Germany in the centralized and mechanized industrial organization that makes for military might. The United States, however, has no huge mechanized neighbor next door: people here can afford more decentralization, a gentler pace of living. Moreover, as Stuart Chase and Lewis Mumford have pointed out, the old coal-and-steam concentrations of the machine age are giving way to the natural decentralization of the hydroelectric age: high-tension transmission lines mean that factories can be set up along a railroad siding anywhere, which gives even the lowest-income belt-line worker a fighting chance to avail himself of the Borsodi short cuts to small ownership of productive property in the country. Barring war and a consequent major catastrophe for America, the technological trend of the century favors the decentralists.

In any event a comprehensive design for national living does not necessarily have to sacrifice either the benefits of centralization or decentralization: the fact that automobiles can be made more cheaply by mass production is no argument against Joe Doakes's desire to raise cabbages and strawberries for himself. And the fact that Mrs. Doakes likes to can her own tomato juice ensures a steady job for someone who takes his pay from the centralized Ball fruit-jar interests.

The truth is that society is generally a state of tension between centripetal and centrifugal forces. Only yesterday the Cassandras and Jeremiahs were bewailing the "doom" of the family-unit farm. But in the recent twenty-fifth anniversary issue of *The New Republic*, Secretary of Agriculture Henry A. Wallace assured us that mechanization does not by any means doom the small farmer. Small tractors, small combines and other small-scale labor-saving machines should enable the little fellow to compete with the big fellow in most parts of the country this side of the arid High Plains and north of the Texas-Oklahoma cotton belt. The power-age should enable us to have it both ways: centralization and "as if" competitive pricing in the huge basic industries that require huge investments and working capital, decentralization and freedom in the smaller industries, trades and aptitudes. We have been gloomily celebrating the demise of the Jeffersonian ideal in America; but even as the echoes of Cassandra and Jeremiah die away there is a streak of light in the eastern sky.

The Total Frame

SOME years ago I lived for a summer in an old—well, relatively old—house at Douglaston, Long Island, that was redolent of the decade that bears the stamp of Theodore Roosevelt. The house had belonged to a popular magazine illustrator who stood somewhere between Charles Dana Gibson and Leyendecker in ability; his innocent, boyish pictures still adorned the walls, and the bookshelves were filled with the lighter titles of an age that had relaxed with F. Hopkinson Smith and furrowed its brows over Winston Churchill and David Graham Phillips. I remember being puzzled by the house in Douglaston. Like everyone else who came of age in the twenties, I had been reading books by Ludwig Lewisohn, H. L. Mencken and others whose stock in trade was complaining of the cultural sterility, the flatness, the dreariness, of life in pre-war America. Here, in this house, everything to which the Lewisohns and Menckens objected had been preserved. Only it didn't seem in the least flat and dreary; it was, on the other hand, fragrant with some ill-defined hope.

Since I was busy that year with a book on the pre-war Progressive movement, I spent the summer consciously sorting out the hopes and the promises of the Rooseveltian decade. The light confidence expressed by that house in Douglaston was, I decided, an extremely passive phenomenon: the confidence of a people that trusted to the luck of events for happiness and not to the strength of their own arms. The electric-light bulb, the early phonograph, the telephone, the automobile—all the new machine-age contrivances which had arrived quite without effort on the part of the average man had resulted in an Aladdin's-lamp view of the future. This view was conceived as an extension of the past, for America, traditionally, had been the land of milk and honey. Side by side with the passive general hope there went a more active political hope: a people that had been disturbed by the revelations of the muckrakers were inclined, when they thought about it, to put their faith in the election of "good" men to office. The "good" man, in the Rooseveltian decade, was the trust-buster, one who would return to the small competitor the control of the American industrial machine that was so prolific of light bulbs, phonographs, telephones and automobiles. But this political hope in the trust-buster —the one positive hope of the decade—was not shared by all those who were vaguely expectant of a fine American future: there was plenty of the let-well-enough-alone spirit abroad in the land that made William Howard Taft President in 1909.

I was very conscious, of course, that the light optimism of the pre-war years had been attacked with good reason by scores of young critics—the young Mumfords,

the young Randolph Bournes, the young Waldo Franks
—in the Wilsonian decade. And I was conscious, too,
that sometime before 1912 the inner-circle Rooseveltians, who had shaken the big stick at the trusts in 1906
and 1907, had with equally good reason decided that
concentration was here to stay in heavy industry, and
that control, not pulverization, must henceforward be
the Progressive watchword. But, as an historian, I was
trying to pin down the exact dates of mutation. Where,
in the years before 1912, was the prophetic voice, the
harbinger of the swelling chorus of the later critical
awakening? And whence came the first positive realization that trust-busting wasn't enough? True, there were
socialists around in the Rooseveltian decade, but their
prophecies depended less on fresh native insight than
on a hand-me-down critique of British and European
capitalism. There were the muckrakers, such as Steffens, who had lost hope in a reversionary recapture of
primitive capitalism. There were Populists, La Follet-
tians, Bryanites, Fabians, Single Taxers, Anarchists,
what-not. But none of them, so far as I know, con-
tributed any real critical analysis of the nature of the
hopes and promises which to the vast majority of
Americans were as natural as blood-pressure. And none
of them, in consequence, was in a position to strike home
with a message capable of absorption.

I didn't get around to reading Herbert Croly's "The
Promise of American Life" during that summer in
Douglaston. And when I did read Croly a year later I

was off on a different tangent: I had become a *pro-tem* hand-me-down Marxian myself. "The Promise of American Life" had been published in 1909, in the high noon of the period whose hopes had fascinated me in that house in Douglaston. But all I could see during my first reading of Croly was his habit of seeking refuge in phrases such as "national interest" and "the nationalization of reform." In writing about Croly in "Farewell to Reform," I complained of a lack of concrete proposals, of "rumination in the upper air." Croly's mystical vision of the "nation" organized for progressive purposes made little sense to me, for I was chiefly impressed at the time with the vital differences that prevent groups or classes from achieving a "concert." Croly had written about the need for "sincerity" in politics; but talk of the "national interest" or "the nationalization of reform" seemed to me an insincere way of fudging issues. One man's "national interest" is notoriously the next man's poison. What the "promise of American life" was to Herbert Croly eluded me completely.

Since that time I have gone back to "The Promise of American Life" on more than one occasion. Although its persistent abstractedness still drives me wild if I read it for any extended period, I have come to think of it as a far more important book than I realized in 1932. My original trouble with it is not far to seek: I tried to take it on a 1932 basis, and was consequently looking for a quality of final awareness that cannot in the nature of things be part of any pioneer's book. And in looking for a superhuman Croly, I missed the one prophetic voice that would have connected those queer, hopeful pre-war years with the sharply critical and disillusioned years that followed. Croly put no faith in trust-busting. And he expressed "an active and intense dislike of the [average American's] mixture of optimism, fatalism and conservatism"—a mixture that resulted in "the expectation that the familiar benefits [of American life] will continue to accumulate automatically." There, in a few abstract phrases, the import of that house in Douglaston was made doubly plain: the pictures on the walls, the books on the shelves, were alike in being products of a culture that expected a continual fall of manna from heaven in spite of the fact that the power to produce was drifting, despite the trust-busters, into progressively fewer hands. Croly, in 1909, had put his finger on all that was weak in the American character— and had done it before anyone else.

At a time when John Dewey was still struggling with the implications of his version of the pragmatic philosophy, Herbert Croly was already a full-fledged instrumentalist. To him, the real promise of American life could only be achieved by the double activity of taking thought for the morrow and by conscious political organization to attain the ends defined in that thought. Pragmatism, or instrumentalism, has been criticized as a "prostrate" philosophy by Waldo Frank and

Lewis Mumford, but there was nothing prostrate about Croly, whose "thought for the morrow" was always based on certain values that were, for him, beyond argument. The "promise" of American life was a democratic promise. Croly was a democrat in that he believed in representative institutions. But he was an aristocrat in his passionate hope—see his essay on the character of Lincoln—that democrats could be taught to put their political trust in the hands of exceptional men. Whether there is a real paradox here, I doubt; democracy must have leadership.

Herbert Croly's parents had been followers of August Comte, whose positivism had made a religion of science. Born with the spoon of rationalism sticking from his mouth, Herbert Croly was from the beginning a samurai-hunter, a believer in a society whose opportunities would bring the wise and the good to the top. In this sense he was not an equalitarian. And, quite naturally, he detested the Jeffersonian tradition in politics. Jeffersonians flattered the people even when the people should be criticized; they courted favor for votes; they were enemies of effective government. Moreover, their philosophy of decentralization could not be acted upon in an age that saw Andrew Carnegie barricading himself at Skibo Castle behind a rampart consisting of a first mortgage on the U. S. Steel Corporation. There was no hope in 1909 that the extremities of the nation could govern themselves democratically without firm co-ordination from the center.

The American Stakes

Croly's pronounced anti-Jeffersonian bias set him apart from the "one-thing-is-enough" reformers of his time—from the Bryanites and the Populists, whose shibboleth was cheap money; from the Single Taxers, whose one Open Sesame was a drastic fiscal reform; from the trust-busters, whose be-all and end-all was a Federal Trade Commission with real wolf's teeth. A Hamiltonian, Croly wanted a central government equipped to run the United States as a unit, with power to move in a co-ordinated way on all fronts at once. "In becoming responsible for the subordination of the individual to the demand of a dominant and constructive national purpose," he wrote, "the American state will in effect be making itself responsible for a morally and socially desirable distribution of wealth."

That sentence can stand as typical of the Croly style —which, in its rambling abstractedness, is enough to keep a semanticist busier than a bird-dog in an aviary. Lifted from its context, such a sentence could frighten the daylights out of me: the argument of the fascist is that his state "subordinates" the individual to a "dominant and constructive national purpose." But Croly, although he regarded Jefferson as responsible for "that career of intellectual lethargy, superficiality and insincerity which ever since has been characteristic of official American political thought," was careful to define his "dominant and constructive national purpose" in at least quasi-Jeffersonian terms. He admitted that Hamilton had "perverted the American national idea almost as much as Jefferson perverted the American democratic idea."

Croly was, in brief, a believer in Jefferson's ends and Hamilton's means—although he never phrased his credo succinctly. Personally, I think "The Promise of American Life" wrongs Jefferson at many points. It is true that Jefferson's two terms in office were largely do-nothing terms. But during his presidency Jefferson had the Napoleonic wars to contend with—and we all know by now just how difficult it is to carry through a democratic program at home when the rest of the world is organized for destruction. Jefferson himself was quite aware of his failure as President; he admitted it when he spoke of the Declaration of Independence and the University of Virginia as his real monuments. The failure, however, had little to do with the subsequent "lethargy, superficiality, and insincerity," of latter-day American political thought. These unlovely characteristics derived from facts in the external world —from the richness of the new American continent, which made political thought largely unnecessary for almost a hundred years. "Sincerity" returned to politics in Croly's day because the "automatic" benefits of nature were running thin. The blame for the "insincerity" of Grant and Coolidge can only be pinned to Jefferson if we are willing to condemn him for tempting millions of Americans with the fat lands acquired by the Louisiana Purchase. But on Croly's own nationalistic premises such condemnation would be fantastic.

The American Stakes

With its Hamiltonian emphasis on central machinery and its Jeffersonian bias in favor of opportunity for the common man, "The Promise of American Life" was a "natural" for the Rooseveltians of 1912. Roosevelt himself read "The Promise" with a leaping brain—and from its pages came the slogans and the program of the Bull Moose "New Nationalism." That "new nationalism" differed from Woodrow Wilson's "new freedom" in one thing: its attitude toward the trusts. When the Progressives assembled at Chicago in 1912, ready for their famous Armageddon, they had first of all to settle a private quarrel among themselves. There was a long struggle behind the scenes over an anti-trust plank, but in the end the forces that believed in the regulation, as against the pulverization, of concentrated economic power won the day. The economic atomizers were forced into the Wilsoniam camp—where they shortly discovered Wilsonian trust-busting to be as feeble as the T.R. 1907 variety.

In recognizing the impossibility of breaking down giant agglomerations such as U. S. Steel into little competing pieces, Croly was ahead of his time. Nor, as we have seen, has the quarrel been finally settled to this day: when the New Deal came along a quarter of a century after the New Nationalism and the New Freedom, it was shaken by the same old conflict that had split Progressives back in 1912. But even the trust-busters among the New Dealers—the disciples of Louis Brandeis and Felix Frankfurter—were forced to admit the impossibility of unmerging the heavier industries by political fiat: competition might be enforced in certain businesses, but steel, copper, aluminum, the railroads—all the industries requiring tremendous capital outlays—must be "controlled" through their pricing policies. Thus the economic prophet in Croly has been vindicated by the tide of events. But only partially vindicated: for pricing control aimed at cheapness, or "as if" competition, is more of a Brandeisean than a Crolyesque means.

Events have vindicated Croly's criticism of American political institutions, as well. Croly believed in limited government, in the reservation and full guarantee of certain rights to states, to minorities and to the individual. But he did not believe in the stultifying check-and-balance theory that gives an executive a merely nominal power to carry out the deliberative will of the majority. Of the power of the Supreme Court Croly wrote in 1909: "A very small percentage of the American people can in this respect permanently thwart the will of an enormous majority, and there can be no justification for such a condition on any possible theory of popular Sovereignty." Croly foresaw a time to come when "government by lawyers" "would merely excite a crisis . . . and strengthen the hands of the more radical critics of the existing political system." But the obstruction of legalistic constitution-chopping was not the only check-and-balance evil to be feared. "The American people," so Croly wrote, "have much more to fear

277

from congressional usurpation than they have from executive usurpation. Both Jackson and Lincoln somewhat strained their powers, but for good purposes, and in essentially a moderate and candid spirit; but when Congress attempts to dominate the executive its objects are generally bad and its methods furtive and dangerous. . . ."

Whether the Court-packing plan and the foreign policy of Franklin D. Roosevelt were offered in a "moderate and candid spirit" is, of course, an arguable matter. Nevertheless, Congress as well as the Supreme Court has been guilty during the two terms of the New Deal of attempted usurpation of power—and that Croly could have predicted the "inevitable" conflicts of the Thirties gives "The Promise" a special piquancy for moderns who are looking for fruitful perspectives on American history.

A good deal of "The Promise" has, of course, become the commonplace coin of modern political liberalism. Croly's remark about the non-union man being an "industrial derelict" is beyond argument for all those who think that the power of labor must be built up if we are to have a true democratic balance, or "concert," of the classes. Most of the suggestions for "reconstruction" in "The Promise" can be checked against the actual accomplishments of both the Wilsonian and Franklin D. Roosevelt decades. None of these accomplishments could have been brought to pass by Jeffersonian

States' Righters. And—since Progressivism is a matter of running twice as fast to stay in the same place—none of the Croly proposals has been fundamental enough to set our economic house to rights. "The Promise" must be read, then, for its expression of an attitude, not for a program good for all time. But Croly, who was a humble personality, would be the last to claim eternal validity for any of his proposals. He would have welcomed the New Deal as a partial expression of his Jeffersonian-ends-cum-Hamiltonian-means philosophy. But, having put himself behind Roosevelt as against Landon and the Liberty League, he would most certainly have gone on to qualify and criticize the actual New Deal performance.

Whether he would have remained an unmitigated Hamiltonian centralist is itself a matter for conjecture. Since he was obviously neither a socialist nor an advocate of laissez-faire, I think he would have come out eventually for the mixed system whose virtues I will shortly celebrate. We have passed the point where one can be either wholly Hamiltonian or wholly Jeffersonian as to means: the democratic way of life demands a mélange of methods, with various types of industries taken in terms of special individual requirements. To argue for government ownership or control of the TVA dynamos is, for example, not at all the same thing as arguing for government registration of white leghorn chickens. Philosophies of centralization or decentralization must be put forward in this year of Stalin, Hitler

and Wendell Willkie with precise demarcations; else
the "either-or" boys will twist you beyond recognition,
making you into a Fascist, a Communist or a Rugged
Individualist, as suits their demagogic convenience. The
"promise of American life" still requires forethought
and institutional organization, even as Croly wrote in
1909. But the mechanics, the instrumentation, necessarily differ from age to age. Our era is actually discovering the necessary instruments for its *pro tem* salvation.
But our philosophers lag behind events—with the result that men and women seeking to do what must be
done wander in a mist, taking one step forward and two
steps sideways. With their attention divided and distracted, they do lamely and unconvincedly what they
should be doing with all their hearts. To break the intellectual log-jam, to provide new frames of reference
for a new generation, we need new Crolys, new social
philosophers with the over-all view into which men can
fit themselves and feel at home doing what must be
done.

We are all a shell-shocked generation. One by one,
as the world stumbled in war or creaked at the joints
because of the chalk-deposits of a capitalism that seemed
irreversibly to be running toward monopoly, we created
our compensatory private Utopias. Regardless of quarrels between gradualists and revolutionists, nearly all
of us had some neat blue-print labeled "socialism," or
"communism," or "basic communism" (Lewis Mum-

ford's contribution), or "planned collectivism" (Max Lerner's), or "co-operative commonwealth" (Alfred Bingham's), tucked away in the back of our minds. We were, in very truth, "escaping" in the name of "realism," forgetting that new institutions always grow out of old institutions, that society never succeeds in breaking cleanly with its past, that no sound or workable systems are or ever can be "pure." And one by one, as the great single modern example of a society created to blue-print order fumbles in the Finnish swamps or shoots its generals, we are turning in revulsion from our escapist illusions. The more intellectualized among us squabble over who turned first: a Benjamin Stolberg or a Eugene Lyons who leaped from the train in 1934 or 1935 cannot forgive a Vincent Sheean or a Ralph Bates for jumping as late as 1939; and in our intense preoccupation with the personalities of a confused transitory period we fall into the habit of always arguing *against*. But sometime we must begin to argue *for*. And that *for* must be expressed in something more than the old and sterile alternatives of individualism versus socialism, or of laissez faire versus "planned collectivism."

In this book my own arguments have been a mixture of negative and positive. I have stated the case against state socialism, which effectively denies the right of an individual to make a living if he fails to please the political party in control of the means and materials of production. I have discussed the fatal weaknesses of anarchism and the lesser weaknesses of Guild Socialism. I have praised the attempts of the Henderson New Deal school to foster an "as if" competitive climate in the big mass industries. I have stated the case for consumer co-operation. I have praised Mr. Ralph Borsodi's practical devices to increase the base of small ownership of productive property—but I have been unwilling to stake more than ten per cent of my hopes upon them. But none of this gets to the nub of the matter. For what I want to do is to hymn the virtue of a mixed economy, an eternally pluralistic economy, not in terms of presenting an argument for chaos or the status quo, but in terms of indicating the proper components of a permanently workable dynamic balance. I am not advocating anything very exciting or original: most of the gentle people who think vaguely of a "middle" way between communism and fascism already believe as I do. But the glamor of the all-or-nothing approach to our social problems must be exposed for the shoddy tinsel that it is.

The place to begin is with our verbal habits, which consistently lead us into making "either-or" analyses and distinctions which have no one-to-one correspondence with the simple facts of life. After centuries of churchly domination the human race persists in carrying over into its secular discussions the polar distinctions of angel-devil, heaven-hell, Christ and anti-Christ. Until very recently most liberals or progressives would have agreed that Soviet Russia was the greatest laboratory experiment in the cause of human betterment that the world has ever seen. Yet how many of us realize that Soviet Russia collapsed long ago, in 1928, and all because of the verbalism of an "either-or" secular priestcraft that let its words become fetishes instead of using them as tools of description and communication?

People don't consume "capitalism" or "socialism"; they consume production. This Lenin understood when he introduced his New Economic Policy, or NEP, in the starveling war-torn Russia of 1921. Under NEP the Soviet State kept control of the "big" things: the railroads, the mines, the new power stations and transmission lines. Thus the industries that normally run the gamut from competition to monopoly in a few short decades were prevented from developing a too dynamic hunger for capital that would have resulted in a new Russian colonialism, with power passing from the locality to British, French and American bankers. But in all the lesser spheres of economic activity the individual was allowed to become a capitalist. And in these spheres Russia commenced to burgeon with no soul-destroying prod from any banker. The NEP years evade statistical tabulation. But the books of Walter Duranty, William Henry Chamberlin and Eugene Lyons tell the story: Russia during the NEP was in process of becoming rich, comfortable—and free. Moscow in 1921 was, according to Duranty, a doleful city; but within two or three

years the Tverskaya had blossomed with private stores
and restaurants, and children walked up and down with
trays of matches, cigarettes, fruit and cakes. Peddlers
abounded; novels and poems were written; Soviet
schoolboys kept amusing diaries; gamblers came out of
hiding—and all was "vulgar, profiteering, crude and
noisy." But the gamblers and debauching were, in Duranty's words, merely the scum on a flood that contained rich silt.

Duranty remembers a Finn selling food for a restaurant table in Moscow. In October of one year the Finn
was working on his own. Six months later the Finn had
become a middleman employing four salesmen. A year
after entering business the Finn sold out to a co-operative; but he had $20,000 or $30,000 in his pocket.

Orthodox communists must regard this Finn as a terrible creature. And so he was, according to the tenets of
an abstract socialism. But the point Duranty makes is
that the Finn stimulated peasants to fatten chickens and
pigs, to grow vegetables, to make wooden bowls and
platters and spoons and clay pots. The same thing was
happening all over Russia; in Samara, you could see
peasants buying locally-produced nails, sandals, cooking utensils, sheepskin coats, baskets, even cottage-made
shoes plaited from osier. The vast majority of peasants
were busy working land of their own as Bukharin's
"Enrich yourselves" quieted their fears of expropriation. Only a few *batraks*, or landless peasants, were on
the outside looking in.

All this burst of activity which put fat into the Soviet camel's hump was anathema to followers of Stalin and Trotsky alike. For Lenin, the great Lenin, had said in 1921: "We are now making a strategic retreat." In other words, collectivism and not production had been made the test of NEP, which naturally damned it from the start. The class that brought NEP to its flowering was doomed to be taxed to death in 1928 and after, when the Five-year planners decreed that most of Russia's energies must be devoted to the making of producer's goods for industrialization.

I go into the NEP phase of the Soviet experience at some length because it has generally been forgotten. Its meaning, however, will loom larger as the Russian revolutionary flame dies away and the country sinks into bureaucratic sloth. NEP succeeded in that it brought a great nation bounding up from famine levels in a few short years. It could not have resulted in "exploitation" of the community, for it is virtually impossible to achieve a monopoly of cabbages and wooden bowls. If the Communists had been scientific planners, instead of "scientific socialists," they would have learned fast in 1921-28. They would have said to themselves: "This NEP isn't pure socialism. But it works quite well in the handicraft-vegetable area of the economy, where no bottlenecks can be seized by bold entrepreneurs. Now let's get on to steel mills without disturbing NEP for the peasants." The Gosplanners would have been compelled to accept a slower pace of industrialization, for men would have been loath to leave the countryside for a collective adventure in the iron-and-coal basins beyond the Urals, nor would they have been willing to give away any large amount of grain to the government to pay for foreign industrial equipment. But a more leisurely tempo on the industrial front would have enabled the Gosplanners to do without forced grain collections and the subsequently necessary drive to sovietize the farms. There would have been no agrarian sabotage, no 1932-33 famine, no wholesale destruction of cattle, horses, chickens.

It is quite true that planners must think in terms of a broad picture; you cannot plan for the parts with no regard for the whole. But planners must also think in institutional terms of what a given plan will do to the spirit of the men involved. The Russian Gosplanners had a nice, broad picture of a swiftly industrialized Commune stretching from the Baltic to the Pacific. They correctly assumed that the creation of steel plants and electric power stations involved corporate activity— or, in Russian terms, state trust activity. "Little" men can't build steel mills: the job is a collective one even under laissez-faire capitalism. But little men *can* make wooden bowls, manage restaurants and plant cabbages. And, having once been given their heads, they cannot be jerked back into an over-all collectivism with impunity. Discontinuous statecraft is unfair statecraft—and as the Russian Gosplanners are still finding out, it usually ends in disaster. And, anyway, maybe cabbages ought always to be left to little men.

David Cushman Coyle has spoken of the several economic systems that exist side by side even under the dispensation known as "finance" capitalism. There is the economic system of small, individualist ownership. There is the economic system of the giant corporation that requires large blocks of capital. There is the economic system of the public utilities—the "natural" monopolies of railroads, central power stations, telephone companies. There are the government collectivisms of the Post Office, the TVA—and a hundred different bodies and agencies and commissions that distribute perquisites and purchasing power to employees. Finally, there is private collectivism: the country club and the Y.M.C.A. and the university are good examples of one kind; the consumer and marketing co-operatives are examples of another.

Marxian analysis assumes (it does not prove) that these five economic systems cannot permanently exist side by side. I assume (I cannot prove) that they must exist side by side if the energies of man are to have the varied scope that they demand. I will admit that the varying uneven rates of development (or retardation) of the five systems can make for serious price and production and investment dislocations. But the "contradictions" of capitalism do not necessarily demand an apocalyptic, final resolution: there can be a series of small, interstitial, *pro tem* resolutions. Dialectic materialism can be given a pluralistic as well as a monistic dress—if we *must* use the harsh gibber of the Marxists.

Looking at the various co-existent economic systems with the claims of the entire community in mind, the following observations become pertinent:

1. The small, individual proprietor—the Iowa corn-hog farmer, the owner of the Pittsburgh Pirates—cannot hold up the community, for this small proprietor cannot achieve a monopoly of food or of entertainment. He may need protection against monopolists in other sectors of the total economy, but that is another story. The point here is that he can't level a gun of his own at anyone's head: he should, therefore, be left alone provided he doesn't commit a public nuisance by letting his topsoil blow away or by selling unhygienic hot-dogs in the bleachers.

2. The great corporation can hold up the community. Since it ordinarily requires great chunks of investment and working capital, it is in a position to out-compete later arrivals in the field before they can get a good running start. Usually the giant corporation sits on the sources of supply, as U. S. Steel sits on the Mesabi Range and Birmingham's iron mountain. Because of these factors, government, as agent for the small man who is certainly numerous enough to put his impress on the State if he keeps his wits about him, might well demand a voice in the pricing policies of the

big corporations if they won't listen to Leon Henderson's plea to "administer" their own prices in the interests of volume sales. There might even be a tax on bigness, graded according to percentage of business done in a given field. As we have seen, some New Dealers have toyed with this idea.

3. The public utility, or natural monopoly, is already under government control, either directly, as in the case of municipal power plants and water works, or indirectly, through commission regulation. Mr. Wendell Willkie, as spokesman for individualism and free competition, ought therefore to find himself a competitive industry; his words come lamely from a man who runs a huge natural monopoly.

4. Government collectivisms which deal in goods and services are of two kinds. The Post Office, for example, must be centrally administered. The TVA, on the other hand, must be administered in the light of local needs. Planners in Washington are competent to draw up a loose general plan for the soil conservation of a continent; they are not competent to tell just what equipment is necessary to plant soil-holding lespedeza on local Tennessee hillsides. The experimentation and decisions needed to carry out a local phase of soil conservation must be made on the spot, as TVA Director David Lilienthal has discovered.

5. Private collectivism should not be mistaken for socialism, or even for a half-way stop on the way to socialism. When farmers band together to market their

produce, or when city individuals start a co-operative restaurant, they are not giving up their individualism. They are, on the other hand, protecting it by trying to get more out of their individual capital equipment or individual income.

General observation: freedom dwells in the interstices of the five economic systems. If you are discarded by U. S. Steel, you may have to fight to start a small business of your own or to get on the government payroll. But you at least have a fighting chance. When a general or a kulak is discarded by the Russian party that controls *all* the means of production, it means exile or death. There must be cross-over possibilities if a nation is to keep the general atmosphere of freedom.

With distinctions between the five economic systems in mind, it should become possible to plan for a total economic area without violating the inner laws of various ways of creating and distributing wealth. The New Deal has in general respected the autonomy of great natural economic divisions: it has not treated the farmers either as serfs or monopolistic plutocrats, nor has it treated Mr. Willkie as a small shop-keeper in a competitive trade. But the New Deal has failed in its functions of mechanical stabilizer and prime mover. Five separate economic systems can and will continue to exist side by side. But there must be a dynamic balance between these systems: steel workers cannot long remain out of work and still buy the farmers' products—not even though the farmers sell through cost-saving (and price-cutting) marketing co-operatives. Always in the past the government has fulfilled a linked dynamic and gyroscopic need: from the Eighteen-sixties to the early Nineteen-hundreds it gave away the public domain, thus subsidizing new producers and consumers and providing an impetus to the nation as a whole. From 1900 on, the separate states began building macadam and concrete highways: this provided the "ladder" upon which the famous automobile ladder industry mounted to its dominant position. But today our imaginations fail; we expect our economy to move without a prime mover. And as we flounder we talk of the need to plan on an "inter-industry" level. But we don't need to get that complicated about the problem: all we need is a new prime mover and a plan for its utilization.

The discovery of such a prime mover should not be difficult. As George Soule and John T. Flynn and Phil La Follette and Eliot Janeway have all pointed out, the rebuilding of the railroads would be a good substitute for a Homestead Act. The railroads are natural monopolies and do not belong to the competitive system anyway. Why not single them out for special treatment as Ohio and North Carolina once singled out their automobile highways? If our stereotypes are against "government ownership" (and they are: witness the fate of Tom Amlie), let Washington force a general writing down of railroad capital claims. The result would be railroad profits—and large-scale modernization of equipment. This would hurt some owners of common stocks and even some owners of bonds. But so does the invocation of Eminent Domain "hurt" a farmer who has a few square feet clipped from his woodlot by a new scenic highway whose vistas leave him quite, quite cold.

As I say, I am not arguing for anything very original or new. My main hope is to help pull our social philosophers back from the all-or-nothing brink upon which they have been teetering for years. These social philosophers are not many in number. But they set the tone of thinking in magazines that are read by key figures in Congress, in newspaper offices, in the colleges. A Max Lerner talking of "planned collectivism" may have it clearly set in his own mind that he is alluding to a program for the Aluminum Corporation of America and not to New Jersey tomato growers or a Third Avenue antique shop proprietor. But his terminology has just enough flavor of the inclusive to scare the antique shop proprietor out of his wits when he reads an echo of Mr. Lerner in a labor party politician's speech. The practical consequences of this may be felt when the antique shop proprietor votes himself and his whole family against a measure designed to free the railroad equipment industries and the steel mills. The same unfortunate consequences may flow from Professor George Counts' failure to discuss the plural economic bases of individual freedom in a book devoted to a treatment of democracy. Ditto for Alfred Bingham's failure to distinguish clearly between property rights making for freedom and property rights making for corporate monopoly.

We are, however, only at the beginning of a turn in the cycle of social thought. It is important that Herbert Agar, Arthur Garfield Hays, Maury Maverick, Mordecai Ezekiel, Max Lerner, George Soule, George Counts and Alfred Bingham have all recently written books that reveal an increasing suspicion of Marxist stringency. The iron "law of motion" which Marx thought he discerned in the capitalist system no longer bemuses our intellectuals; they are ready to put it in a bin that contains the rejected "iron law of wages" of the early Victorian economists. It may be true that the new "democracy" books fail generally to come clean on the question of the relations between freedom and private ownership of certain of the means and materials of production. (Herbert Agar is the only one of the crowd to take a firm position here.) But none of the new democracy books is final in any sense. All we can say is that a ferment is working and that our social philosophers are going native once more; inclusive systematizing will come later. Meanwhile, if Russia still rests on our consciences, let us take the NEP Russia for a pointer reading; let us assume that Russia went wrong in 1928 when she "planned" without regard for human factors in one important type of economic activity. If we must talk in Russian terms, let us speak of moving towards a "permanent NEP." But let us keep this language to ourselves, for NEP was Jeffersonian before it was Russian, and there is no reason to go abroad to look for the native article.

The attitude which I have been advocating in these pages comes naturally enough to those of us who grew up before the Great Depression of 1929. The young, however, must be converted; and since the young have the zeal and are already on the collectivist band-wagon it is going to be difficult to bring them back into the progressive mainstream of American life. Open polemics will be useless; the economic system itself must be expanded to take the young in and give them jobs. Democracy, the freedom of five economic systems each offering cross-over possibilities to the dissatisfied, must prove itself by works, not words. If you don't believe it, take a look at my friend Andy Perkins, who used to work in an office down the corridor from me. Two years ago Andy was an office boy, a bright one who had hopes of writing. He had been, at an incredibly youthful age, both an organizer for the C.I.O. in eastern Pennsylvania and a communist, and as an office boy he took a deeply earnest interest in the local chapter of the American Newspaper Guild. Andy regarded me as a benighted liberal, a person with—maybe—a good heart but with just a little too much income to stay put on the radical side of the fence. I used to have fun arguing with Andy. You could actually get him on the subject of his political affiliation, for he was quite willing to admit that communists in Russia had scant regard for civil liberties, for political democracy, or for the legal traditions of those countries which Professor George Catlin has lumped together under the larger heading of "Anglo-Saxony." But Andy always returned stubbornly to the same point. "A young fellow's got to believe that his life is coming to something," he used to say. "This economic system is never going to spread out enough to take us all in. You liberals, the New Deal and all that, can give us something. But only enough to make us ask for more. If we succeed in getting a living wage by reformist political measures, why should we be content to stop there?"

Thus argued Andy Perkins for a few months after he had ceased to be an office boy. He was despairful at the time of ever making the grade as a magazine writer, although his education had been sufficient to arouse his sustained curiosity about a great number of things. But slowly the despair ebbed. Andy's new-found confidence did not alter his beliefs, but you could sense a change of emphasis in his daily living. "You know," he said one day, "I've never known a big personality on the communist Left. They're all too wrapped up in the class war; they haven't time to become broad human beings." Andy had left the Communist Party; its demands on time and energy were getting in the way of both education and vocation. But he still retained all his old interest in the Newspaper Guild.

The American Stakes

The story of Andy Perkins is not offered as typical of modern out-of-school youth; indeed, Andy is about as atypical as he could be. To begin with, he is an intellectual and a New Yorker, which puts him in a very small minority at once. Second, he has been a communist. But Andy's story is instructive, for it dramatizes the difficulty of pinning youth down. Had a sample test interviewer caught Andy in a truthful mood two years ago he would have put him down as a radical anti-democrat who subscribed to all the rigmarole about "boring from within." Had he caught Andy last spring he would have discovered a person whose beliefs were in a state of flux. And two years from now—just where will Andy be then? It all depends on how things break for Andy in his chosen vocation.

Since Andy became a communist at a tender age, we can assume that he was badly educated in the values of democracy. But his story illustrates the weaknesses of the theory that correct education is what is necessary to bind youth firmly to the democratic scheme of things. If Andy gets the breaks, if the economic system expands in the future to give him pride of place, his youthful communism will probably be forgotten in spite of his education. On the other hand, if the economic system continues to contract, Andy will probably go back to his communism—or to some more inchoate form of anti-democratic radicalism. But the point to be made here is that other young people who have had democratic values drilled into them from birth will be with Andy, too. Education is a weak bulwark for democracy if democracy can't deliver the goods in the form of jobs, a future, or just plain hope.

Some time ago I heard Phil La Follette, former governor of Wisconsin, say that a definite fault-line of character divides youth from age in the United States. Phil implied that our out-of-school youth is unstable, apathetic (but maybe preparing to move in a hurry), and unable to derive much comfort from slow parliamentary attempts at meliorism. Sidney Hillman made light of Phil's fears that a psychic "explosion," a *crise des nerfs*, is necessarily coming to America sometime in the Forties, but Sidney Hillman was obviously thinking in terms of mature clothing workers, all of whom have certain skills—or at least a pattern of remembered daily activity upon which to build a political program. Phil's rebuttal was this: given five more years of a contracting or even a static capitalism, then young people who have no pattern of remembered activity will simply stampede. They won't go radical in a way to please socialists or neo-socialists; for they will lack the trade union discipline that is needed for old-line socialist or reformist political activity. Phil La Follette is obviously right when he says that a trapped generation will "explode." And the explosion will come, as it came in Italy and Germany, regardless of education. (Note to readers: for "explosion" read fascism if you like.)

But suppose our economic system rocks along, with production picking up. In that case, out-of-school youth

does offer a real current challenge to educators. There
must be educational opportunities to take up the slack
of a temporary period of unemployment; there must
be education in vocational skills. Above all, there must
be education to sharpen youth's faculty to see a job
where no job has ever existed before. Such education
does not necessarily mean putting youth back into high
school or college. But it does involve the creation or
expansion of night schools, vocational schools, and alert
vocational guidance. And dead end jobs must be
accompanied with training on the side for other jobs.

No census has been taken since 1930. But it is a
reasonable guess that there are 20,500,000 young people in the United States between the ages of sixteen
and twenty-four. Of these, some ten million are in
school. Of the ten million plus that have quit school,
mostly for economic reasons, some seven million have
either full time or part time jobs (with a majority
working full time), and some three million are just
hanging around. The unemployment among out-of-
school youth may be figured thus to be around 40 per
cent (including the time spent on the side-lines by those
with only partial employment). All of which means, of
course, that out-of-school youth has the highest unemployment of any age level in the country.

To know whether the schools have done their part
in preparing young people to make the best of a period
that offers only partial employment to some and mere

hopes for employment to a good many more, we must somehow get inside the collective mind of a whole generation. But a word of caution is in order before we go exploring. Since youth is evanescent, since its problems become merged with the adult problems of a whole economy, a whole civilization, in pretty short order, the achievement of getting inside the collective mind of a generation may not be worth very much three years hence. Back in 1933, for example, we had a boy and girl tramp problem, with thousands of kids in their late 'teens and early twenties taking to the road and the hobo jungle. Had a sample test been taken at the time, we might have predicted the worst for our young people: with one in twenty growing up entirely outside the social system (as some of the more inflamed guesses had it), the dice certainly seemed loaded against our traditional democracy of opportunity. One would have been quite justified on the basis of a 1933 sample test in shaking one's head over the failure of a social system that could not keep young people in school, or even off the brake beams of the through freights.

Yet the period of the "wild children" lasted only for a brief moment. Things are better now than they were in 1933, even for young people. As we shall see, the CCC and the National Youth Administration have thrown life-lines to the most desperate cases. And what with FERA and WPA and AAA and Social Security, homes have ceased to break up. "We have bought our-

The American Stakes

selves time to think," said Mrs. Franklin D. Roosevelt. That goes for youth, too.

What, then, is youth thinking? When I see an eighteen-year-old listening hour after hour as the radio "entertainment" drools on, or when I watch Bobby Riggs playing one of his typically lackadaisical tennis matches, I doubt that youth is thinking at all. But this is obviously the prejudice of an old gaffer in his thirties; after all, Bobby Riggs does manage to win important tournaments against smart players. Back in 1936 and 1937 the American Youth Commission of the American Council on Education interviewed some 13,500 young people between the ages of sixteen and twenty-four in the state of Maryland. What emerges from the report of the commission, "Youth Tell Their Story," is a picture of a generation whose group personality is somewhat recessive and apathetic. But, underneath the protective coloration of diffidence, the youth of the Maryland sample have ideas that are just as well defined as Riggs' tennis game.* Two out of three are convinced that wages are generally too low, which would seem to indicate that the underconsumption theory of a faltering capitalism (the theory that has been most assiduously popularized by the New Deal) has sunk in. The youth that is least inclined to regard *general* wages as too low are the farm boys, but

* For the sake of brevity I will use the present tense in discussing the Maryland sample.

these, nevertheless, are the most inclined to consider their own wages too low. Again, this would seem to argue a high degree of receptivity to the principle of parity of purchasing power for agriculture. Twenty years ago individual youths might have grumbled about their own particular rewards, but would they have complained about wage scales as a whole? One wonders.

But how are wages to be raised from the farm boy's median weekly average of $8.44 and the city boy's average of $13.82? Again, youth's answer here is more or less the answer of the New Deal: 40 per cent believe in government regulation of wages (and a surprising number of young people approved of the NRA), while 22 per cent think labor unions could turn the trick. Only 10 per cent believe in "individual effort," and a mere 4 per cent is for a "new economic system." So much for the extremes of rugged individualism and communism.

It would be easy to argue from these figures that a fair majority of young people are for the democratic "social service" state. Well, they are—and they aren't. They share the fundamental American distrust of "isms," but they believe government should, in Leon Henderson's words, "do what it takes." On the other hand, they tend to be cynical about the suffrage. Fifty-five per cent consider that candidates are elected to office for reasons of "political pull," or "money, graft and bribery." Seventeen per cent answered: "Political

301

machine." Only 5 per cent believe that "personality" can elect a candidate to public office.

Is it paradoxical that this youth that is cynical about democratic processes can also believe in government regulation of wages and hours, central administration of relief (90 per cent regard relief as a valid concern of Washington), and government regulation of child labor? Perhaps it is. Or perhaps it merely proves that American youth is pragmatic, willing to let the "crooked" politicians vote (under penalty of removal from office) for legislation that will benefit the masses. After all, one can regard one's ward boss as a double-dyed rascal, and one's senator as a fathead and still prefer them to the self-chosen "elite" of a dictatorship.

On the basis of the Maryland sample test, youth itself considers economics to be the essence of the "youth problem." Two thirds of the sample voted "economic security" as "youth's own problem," and almost 60 per cent think "economic security" is synonymous with the "youth problem in general." "Education, vocational choice" trails far behind as a chosen category; only 13 per cent voted for this as "youth's own problem." In other words: "Give us jobs, and we'll let the education follow in due course."

How representative is the Maryland sample? The state itself offers a pretty good cross-section of American conditions as a whole: its westernmost tip is hill country; its northern and central counties consist largely of slightly rolling farm lands, like those of southeastern Pennsylvania or south central Ohio; its Calvert County, where tobacco is raised, has a distinct southern flavor and many Negroes; its "eastern shore" gets its living from salt water and from truck farming; its city of Baltimore is both a manufacturing center and a port; and its Prince George County is a suburb of the national capital at Washington. In all these regions people are divided pretty much as elsewhere into poor and well-to-do, unprivileged and privileged, educationally retarded and college bred. Possibly the "old American" character of most Maryland regions gives a "100 per cent American" touch to the Maryland survey that would not be found, say, in an equivalent sample for New York State or Massachusetts. Generally speaking, however, the Maryland sample percentages conform to national percentages; and we can take the word of accredited statisticians that, as sample tests go, the Maryland survey is entirely trustworthy.

The Maryland sample does not prove that our "democracy of opportunity" is functioning for youth; children from the poorest families tend to get the worst jobs and, moreover, they tend to stay in the worst jobs. Class tends to perpetuate class, an American reality that clashes with traditional American theory. And the least privileged groups tend to produce the most children, meaning that there are more and more of a given helpless class to be gripped by the economic vise. To break this vicious circle of economic determinism, the American Youth Commission advocates "more efficient educational, vocational and recreational programs for *all* youth." Certainly youth itself, on the basis of the Maryland sample, is not overly enthusiastic about existing educational, vocational and recreational opportunities. Young people who manage to stay in school until they are eighteen do discover that education helps in job-getting. But the employment and the income of a young person's father profoundly affect the amount of schooling that a given youth is likely to receive. Here, again, we find the vicious circle of economic determinism working. The selective principle behind the recruiting of high school and college students is distinctly *not* intellectual; it is almost entirely economic. As for vocational guidance in school, it proves helpful *insofar as there is any;* 70 per cent of the young people who have received this guidance are grateful for it. But in most schools there is no attempt at vocational guidance; according to the Maryland report, "when all the youth including those now in school are considered, one still finds that only sixteen out of every hundred have received what they consider helpful vocational guidance from their schools." Looking beyond the Maryland sample, we discover from the studies of Carter Goodrich and other sources that vocational opportunities appear most plentifully where they are least needed, and vice versa. The Great Plains region, the coal plateaus of the southern Appalachians, the old Cotton Belt, all have an excess of births over deaths—

and the fewest jobs, the poorest schooling, and the least adequate vocational guidance in the country. The richest agricultural regions tend to have the best agricultural schools; in marginal farming regions, where it takes a skillful man to get a living from the soil, the young and aspiring farmer finds the most difficulty in acquiring skills. And when the surplus population of the Ozark-Appalachian plateaus, the old Cotton Belt and the Great Plains region is drained into the cities, where there is an excess of deaths over births, it finds itself at a disadvantage in competing with urban youth that knows the way around.

In certain European countries youth has sold itself into state slave-service for a pittance. As Hans Kohn says, the "great personal and creative appeal of autonomous freedom and human comradeship which distinguished . . . the pre-war period" is lost. In Russia, five million young people in the Komsomols are under the strict military discipline of the Communist Party. But youth must eat, and if democracy can't provide jobs, then democratic youth may be expected to go the way of German, Italian and Russian youth.

Democracy's stop-gap answer to the challenge of unemployed out-of-school youth has been the Civilian Conservation Corps and the National Youth Administration. Ever since 1933, the CCC has been taking young men from families on the public relief rolls and placing them—an over-all number of at least 350,000 at any given time since 1935—in forestry, park, and soil erosion camps. The CCC is voluntary, but a candidate must enroll for a minimum service of six months. According to Howard Oxley, 50,000 illiterate boys learned to read and write in CCC camps between 1933 and 1937. Some 300,000 more continued elementary schooling, 200,000 studied high school subjects, and 50,000 took college subjects. Vocationally, the CCC is limited; but it has turned out young men with a useful knowledge of soil conservation, road building, forestry, automobile mechanics, carpentry, furniture-making, and cooking. Not a few youthful truck drivers in private industry owe their jobs to CCC apprenticeship. The National Youth Administration, set up in June of 1935, has not had the funds to take care of more than a mere fraction of the young people who are unemployed or unable to afford vocational school or college. But, for a few hundred thousand boys and girls, it has helped to provide work on locally sponsored projects, and its pay checks have enabled a number of young people to continue their education on at least a part-time basis. Residence projects, which are really co-operative schools, have resulted in a few young people learning how to become farmers, seamstresses and stenographers.

But with three million and more out-of-school youth waiting around for something to turn up, the opportunities for temporary employment and limited vocational training offered by CCC and NYA are obviously not enough. Our mass production economic system demands higher skills from fewer people, whereas our school system has been giving better cultural training in recent years to more people. This results in a scissors, the two blades of which open to create an ever larger area of discontent in between. When more and more of the discontented find themselves with time on their hands and no way to pay for the enjoyments of the good life which school has led them to demand, we are likely to discover ourselves with an ugly and morose younger population—a population with latent potentialities for political evil. Nothing much is being done to prevent the growth of such a phenomenon; and our do-nothingism in this respect is the measure of our democratic failure.

The problem, however, is not a "youth" problem. We come back to the need for a modern substitute for the Homestead Act or the new county and state roads of the early twentieth century. If the people, working through their elected representatives, have the courage and intelligence to provide a new prime mover for the economy, the young will be absorbed into jobs as they come out of school. If that prime mover is not discovered, then youth—not the older unemployed, not the Townsendites—will take on the storm-trooper mentality—and our democracy will disappear.

SELECTED BIBLIOGRAPHY

Agar, Herbert: *Pursuit of Happiness*

Alsop, Joseph and Catledge, Turner: *The 168 Days*

Alsop, Joseph and Kintner, Robert: *Men Around the President*

Beard, Charles A.: *The Open Door at Home*

Belloc, Hilaire: *Economics for Young People* (ENGLISH TITLE: *Economics for Helen*)

Chamberlin, Edward: *The Theory of Monopolistic Competition*

Chase, Stuart: *The New Western Front*

Childs, Marquis: *Sweden: The Middle Way*

Cole, G. D. H.: *The World of Labor*

Croly, Herbert: *The Promise of American Life*

Dangerfield, George: *The Strange Death of Liberal England*

Duranty, Walter: *Duranty Reports Russia*

Duranty, Walter: *I Write As I Please*

Frank, Jerome: *Save America First*

Hallgren, Mauritz: *The Tragic Fallacy*

Kropotkin, Peter: *Fields, Factories and Workshops*

Laski, Harold: *The State in Theory and Practise*

Lyons, Eugene: *Assignment in Utopia*

Nock, Albert Jay: *Our Enemy the State*

Oppenheimer, Franz: *The State*

Russell, Bertrand: *Power: A New Social Analysis*

Russell, Bertrand: *Proposed Roads to Freedom*

Soule, George: *An Economic Constitution for Democracy*

INDEX

Index

Index

313

Index

Index

Index

Index

Index